THE NEW
SUMMIT HIKER
AND SKI TOURING GUIDE

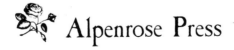 Alpenrose Press

———THE NEW——— SUMMIT HIKER
AND SKI TOURING GUIDE

50 Historic Hiking and Ski Trails
near Breckenridge, Frisco, Copper Mountain,
Keystone-Dillon, in the Williams Fork and
Gore Range Wilderness, Colorado

by Mary Ellen Gilliland

Library of Congress Catalog Card Number: 83-71361

ISBN: 1-889385-07-7
First printing, 1983
Second printing, 1987
Third printing, revised and expanded edition, 1992
Fourth printing, revised edition, 1995
Fifth printing, revised edition, 1997
Sixth printing, revised edition, 1999
Seventh printing, revised edition, 2002

 Alpenrose Press

P.O. Box 499
Silverthorne, Colorado 80498
(970) 468-6273
(970) 468-2080 FAX
e-mail: author@alpenrosepress.com
www.alpenrosepress.com

CONTENTS

LEGEND
For Individual Hike Maps

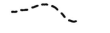 Trail

 Approximate Trail Location or Indistinct Trail

 Trailhead - Park Here

 Road to Trailhead

For you shall go out in joy,
and be led in peace. Is. 55:12

ACKNOWLEDGMENTS

Generous people lent their time and expertise to help launch this book. A hearty "thank you" goes to Jim Gregg, U.S. Forest Service Recreation Forester, Dillon Ranger District, who offered ideas during first-edition planning, guidance during research and his exhaustive trails experience in critiquing the manuscript. Jim Gregg made himself entirely available, always ready to answer questions and solve problems.

Thanks to Breckenridge historian, Maureen Nicholls, who reviewed the Breckenridge area text and hunted through old mining maps to help identify 1800s mine sites.

Tom Jones, of WildernesSports in Silverthorne's Summit Place Shopping Center, shared his intimate knowledge of Summit County's high country, especially of trails in the Gore Range. First edition helpers include Breckenridge mountaineer Rick Hum, and avid hiker, Becky Katovich. The U.S. Forest Service's Bruce Fahrni shared his local trails lore as a manuscript reader. Karen Archer, who introduced us to a number of new trails, waited patiently while notes where scribbled and photos shot.

Gratitude not only for special talent, but also for enthusiasm, goes to copy editors, Jack and Elsa Gilliland. Jan Gregg executed all the book's map work. Michelle Bacon of Breckenridge's Graphic Ink designed the book; Dannette Peterson and Peggy Fallon–Koehn designed later editions. *The Denver Post's* Mike Keefe created the cover illustration.

Contributors to 1992's revised and expanded edition included Tom Healy, Dillon Ranger District; Nancy Redner, hiker and wildflower expert; Leigh Girvin-Yule, Summit Huts and Trails Association; Susan Donaldson, Breckenridge hiker; and Jim and Mil Plant, orienteering experts. For the 2002 edition, Sheliah Gilliland contributed proofreading skills.

To my business manager and computer guy, Larry Gilliland, I give my special thanks.

M.E.G

Above: Exuberance happens on a high ridge when sunny skies and knockout views combine to please cross-country skiers.

U.S. Forest Service signs suggest uses for popular trails, here separating skier/hiker and motorcycle use areas.

HIKES BY DIFFICULTY

EASY

13	Mt. Royal to Masontown
15	Ten Mile Canyon National Recreation Trail
17	Meadow Creek-Salt Lick Gulch
31	Sapphire Point
32	Tenderfoot Mountain
33	Old Dillon Reservoir
36	Lily Pad Lakes
38	Mesa Cortina
45	Lower Cataract Lake

MODERATE

1	Blue Lakes-Monte Cristo
3	McCullough Gulch
5	Mohawk Lakes
7	Indiana Creek
8	Black Powder Pass
16	North Ten Mile
21	Wilder Gulch
26	Loveland Pass West
39	South Willow Falls
42	Rock Creek-Boss Mine
43	Boulder Lake
44	Gore Range Trail

MORE DIFFICULT

4	Wheeler National Recreation Trail
6	Crystal Lake
10	The Mail Run
11	Ten Mile Meadows via upper trailhead
12	Mt. Victoria
14	Mt. Royal Summit
19	Wheeler Lakes
23	Guller Creek on the Colorado Trail
24	Mayflower to Clinton Gulch Loop
25	Mt. Sniktau
29	Chihuahua Gulch
34	Ptarmigan Mountain
41	Willow Lakes
46	Surprise and Tipperary Lakes
48	Eaglesmere Lakes

MOST DIFFICULT

2	Quandary Peak
11	Ten Mile Meadows via Peaks Trail
18	Meadow Creek
20	Uneva Pass
22	Miners Creek
27	Porcupine Gulch
28	Lenawee Trail

HIKES FOR CHILDREN

CROSS COUNTRY SKI TRAILS

BEFORE YOU BEGIN...

All thy works shall give thanks to thee, O Lord. (Ps. 145:10)

The splendor of creation shines forth in snow-capped peaks that scrape the sky, flower-dappled alpine meadows, darkling forest cut by crystal streams. Summit County abounds in nature's beauty and offers a variety of terrain, from fluttering aspen forest through evergreen wood to sun-swept open tundra. Relics from its gold rush days remain to intrigue Summit hikers.

Fifty hikes into Summit County's golden yesterdays are highlighted. There are ten hikes around Breckenridge; eight around Frisco; six around Copper Mountain; eleven around Keystone-Dillon; thirteen in the primitive Gore Range; and two in the Williams Fork Range.

This guide seeks to help hikers avoid getting lost; to provide new trails for both local and visiting hikers to enjoy; to suggest mountain experiences for all levels of hikers, from aggressive to recreational to families with first-time hikers. A companion to Mary Ellen Gilliland's *SUMMIT, A Gold Rush History of Summit County, Colorado,* the book aims to help hikers walk into the county's vivid past.

Each hike has an interesting destination, including waterfalls, lakes, mines, passes, peaks, historic sites and view spots. Trails vary in length, from almost twelve miles to less than one mile. They also vary in elevation. The Argentine Pass route exceeds 13,000 feet in elevation, while the Cataract Lake loop maintains a mild 8,700-foot level.

Do you like *The Summit Hiker?* Try Gilliland's newly-revised hiking, cross-country ski and snowshoe trails guide for neighboring Eagle County, *The Vail Hiker.* (See page 117.)

HOW TO USE THE TRAIL STATISTICS:

Each trail chapter begins with seven facts that describe the hike: Time, distance, elevation gain, high point, rating, season open and topographic map required. Following are explanations for each.

Time: Times estimated refer to a round-trip hike and reflect a walking pace of 2 miles per hour. Time given includes rest stops, lunch breaks and brief exploring jaunts. Each hike's time is modified by trail difficulty and steepness. Individual hikers will set individual paces. The hour figure provides a general goal for hikers to inform family or friends of return time. Hours spent driving to and from the trailhead are not included.

Distance: Mileage is given for one-way only. Sometimes this guide's mileages and on-site trail signs will differ, but usually in no significant way. Distance figures come from trail research, U.S. Forest Service figures and topographic map measurements.

Elevation gain: This number gives hikers a solid base to gauge the trail's difficulty. However, hikers must consider elevation gain together with distance. For example, the stiff Buffalo Mountain Trail climbs almost 3,000 feet in 1.8 miles while the Ptarmigan Mountain hike gains 3,000 feet in 4 miles, a less demanding walk.

High point: The peak elevation on any trail describes the terrain hikers will reach. A lake at 9,800 feet will nestle in green pine forest while a tarn at 11,800 feet may pool below a granite headwall approached by flowery alpine meadows. For visitors from lower elevations, the trail's high point provides a guide for getting acclimated: Begin with below-10,000-foot Tenderfoot Mountain or Lily Pad and work up.

Rating: Many hiking guides shirk trail ratings because individuals evaluate trails in different ways. But most hikers need guidance on the ease or difficulty of the terrain. The rating, though subjective, is therefore included. Criteria for ratings included steepness, trail obstacles or hazards and difficulty in following the path.

Usually open: Snowmelt at extreme altitudes sometimes occurs as late as early July.

Alpine lakes like Chihuahua sometimes (not always) remain frozen July 4 and freeze again in September. Many local back country roads close in May-early June due to soggy spring run-off conditions. However, some trails, like lower-elevation Cataract Lake and south-facing Tenderfoot, open in early June.

Topo map: Topographic maps, a "must" for many of this book's hikes, are available through the U.S. Geological Survey's Central Region Map Distribution Center, Building 810, Denver Federal Center (Box 25286), Denver, Colorado 80225. WildernesSports, in Silverthorne's Summit Place Shopping Center, also carries a complete map supply, along with clothing and gear for hikers.

To read a topographic map, study the contour lines which connect points of equal elevation distanced from sea level. The space between the contour lines, called the contour interval, measures vertical distance. When contour lines crowd close on the map, this indicates steepness. Spaced contour lines evidence more gentle terrain. You can calculate the interval on any topographic map by finding the difference between any two consecutive figures appearing along every fifth contour line and then dividing the figures by five. Check your map: Some use 20-foot intervals, while others use 200-foot intervals. This book's topographic maps, except for the Summit County North and South maps, use a 40-foot interval.

Gray areas on our maps indicate vegetation while white shows above-timberline or open areas.

Many Summit County area USGS maps were photo-revised in 1987 to show recent development. If you don't wish to carry USGS topo maps, purchase the widely-available *Trails Illustrated* maps, which cover large areas and are photo-reduced from USGS maps.

YOUR RUCKSACK:

Map and *compass*--and the ability to use them--are essential. Summit's high altitude allows ultraviolet rays to penetrate clear air, so *sunglasses* are vital, as is *sunscreen* and possibly a long-sleeved shirt. *Insect repellent* comes in handy. Extra *shoes* earn their keep for fording streams and camp wear. Waterproof kitchen *matches*, a signal *mirror* and a pocket *knife* serve many emergency uses, as do a *first aid kit* and *flashlight*. For summer storms, tote a *water-repellent jacket* or *poncho*. For high altitude hikes, especially after September 1, carry a wool *hat* and *gloves*, *sweater* and *wind breaker* and possibly a *down vest*. Don't forget high-energy *snacks* like hard candy, chocolate, dried fruit. Bring *water*. Finally: Always carry a *litter bag*.

EAGLES NEST AND PTARMIGAN PEAK WILDERNESS AREAS:

Seventeen of this guide's hikes penetrate the 133,688-acre Eagles Nest Wilderness, a primitive area in the Gore Range. Three hikes enter the new 13,000-acre-Ptarmigan Wilderness. Certain regulations exist here: Groups are limited to 10; campsites and fires must be located at least ¼ mile from lakes and 100 feet streams and trails to protect sensitive vegetation and water sources; no motorized vehicles or equipment of any kind are allowed; landing of aircraft or air drop of persons or supplies is prohibited. The Forest Service also urges hikers to leave pets at home. If Rover comes along, he must be leashed.

TIPS FOR HIKERS:
Your Safety...

Summit County has a 911 emergency call system. Dispatch a fellow hiker to dial 911 for any emergency.

Altitude sickness first strikes with headache, lack of appetite and nausea.

Avoid hiking alone. If you must, leave trail route and anticipated return time with a family member or friend.

Hypothermia lowers the body core temperature. Give hot drinks (no alcohol) and keep the victim warm and dry.

Even clear cold streams and lakes can harbor *Giardia lamblia*, a nasty organism that attacks the digestive tract. To purify, boil water at least 15 minutes at these altitudes and add iodine according to package directions. Sophisticated chemical purifiers will kill *Giardia*. These germicides contain tetraglycine hydroperiodide and titratable iodine.

Electrical storms above timberline threaten hikers' lives. Lightning strikes and hazardous ground currents are deadly. When you see a thunderstorm brewing, turn back. Avoid electrical storms by starting the hike first thing in the morning. Storms usually begin in the early afternoon.

To warm up before a longer hike, use stretching exercises. Bob Anderson's *Stretching*, Shelter Publications, provides specific hiking warm-ups that can help to prevent problems such as painful inflamed knee cartilage.

The Environment...

At mountain elevations, food waste does not biodegrade. Eggshells, orange peels and other picnic refuse remains. Animals don't eat such foods. Repackage food to lighten your load and eliminate glass and aluminum. Food, wraps and aluminum cans should go in the litter bag. Make sure Kleenex gets back in your pocket. Pack it in--Pack it out!

Outdoor lovers help protect flowers by refraining from picking them and animals by quietly allowing them to pass. Hikers can protect fragile alpine tundra by walking on rocks or snow. Trail erosion is diminished when hikers stay on trails. Avoid short-cutting switchbacks, which forms a path for water erosion. Remind others to stay on the trail, single file, even when it's muddy. Especially during damp periods, hikers can cause havoc to vulnerable forest and alpine terrain.

Campers should use today's lightweight and efficient stoves to avoid a fire ring, which causes an unsightly permanent scar. If a fire is necessary, never cut standing trees. Carry small firewood from timbered areas outside camp. Use biodegradable soaps and wash away from lakes or streams.

Federal law prohibits disturbing historical sites. Don't remove nails, boards or objects.

People once asked "Can man survive in the wilderness?" Today the question has become "Can the wilderness survive man?"

SKI TOURING AND SNOW SHOEING:

Twenty-two trails or trail accesses in this book offer a delightful cross-country ski or snow shoe experience. Summit's powdery snow makes ski touring a physical pleasure, while mountain scenery provides a feast for the spirit. Driving directions for hikers will also bring skiers and snow shoers to winter trailheads.

Remember that steep treeless slopes threaten avalanche danger. Call Colorado Avalanche Information 668-0600 for current data on mountain weather, snow and avalanche conditions 24 hours daily, November 15-May 1. Or visit the U.S. Forest Service office at 680 Blue River Parkway, Silverthorne to obtain avalanche reports. In general, avoid traveling alone, traversing open slopes during or after a blizzard, and count windward slopes as more safe than leeward.

Hypothermia cools the body's core, endangering vital organs. Shivering, slurred speech, tiredness and disorientation are symptoms.

Cross-country skiers and snow shoers at Summit's altitudes require plenty of liquids to offset fluid losses through rapid respiration in dry air. Fluids work to keep skiers warmer as well. Alcohol and smoking shut down the capillaries, restricting blood flow to extremities.

HELP UPDATE THIS BOOK:

Though these 50 trails were researched recently, most hiked in 2001, routes can change when rock slides, washouts or other natural reversals occur. Sometimes officials construct alternate routes or "manage" an area to the detriment of hikers. Examples: Climax Molybdenum Company has closed the access to Searle Gulch and the Kokomo Pass area along the Colorado Tail, eliminating two trails in this book's last edition. Sometimes, hikers themselves will establish or change a trail. Help update, correct or add to this guide. Write to: Alpenrose Press, Box 499, Silverthorne, Colorado 80498.

Hikes Around Breckenridge

1 BLUE LAKES-MONTE CRISTO

Time: 2 hours
Distance: 1.2 miles
Elevation gain: 752 feet
High point: 12,500 feet
Rating: Moderate
Usually open: July-August
Topo: USGS Breckenridge 1970, rev. 1987

This short hike in an historic area packed with early-day mine relics takes you to the brilliant Blue Lakes, high in mineral-rich Monte Cristo Gulch. A heady 11,748-foot starting altitude puts this entire trail above timberline.

Drive 7.9 miles south on Colorado 9 from Breckenridge's Main Street-Park Avenue stoplight (south end of town) toward Hoosier Pass. Turn right onto Blue Lakes Road (No. 850). At the fork, go straight, traveling 2.2 miles on roadway best driven in 4WD and barely o.k. in the family car. Note the nice waterfall on Monte Cristo Creek along the way. Park just below the dam and cross the walkway above the dam to its north end.

The trail begins north of the dam (right), climbing a very steep slope just yards west of the concrete structure. A slightly easier route exists but is difficult to find: Stand on the dam and look for two large, sandy-brown rock outcroppings above the rubble at the dam's north end. The trail passes in front of the second (or westerly) rock, becoming clear at that point. The track, above the lake's north shore, climbs the southwest shoulder of Quandary Mountain on your right, finally heading along the stream in a northwesterly direction.

Find the trail and wind your way through red-twig willow and alpine meadows for a short 0.7 mile walk to two old mine cabins from the Golden Beaver Mine. One structure has collapsed; a second, with its native rock wall intact, stands in disrepair. A road built in the shard leads to a mine at 12,500 feet. Timbers, barrels and fuel containers mark the area at 1.2 miles, although a rock slide has obliterated the old road here.

Look for dwarf blue columbine, blue alpine harebell (bellflower), yellow stonecrop and rosy queen's crown, all alpine zone flowers found above timberline.

The reservoir below contributes to a major water diversion for the thirsty cities of Aurora and Colorado Springs. The water goes beneath the Divide then to Montgomery Reservoir.

Monte Cristo Gulch abounds with mining history. Miners, who first named the lakes "Quandary Lakes", discovered gold here in the 1860s. The Charlie Ross stood on the saddle between Quandary and Fletcher Mountains. On towering 13,614-foot North Star Mountain, rising at the dam's south end, were the Jack Lode with its own ore mill, the Eldorado, Witch Hazel, O'Reilly Group and the famous Arctic Mine. The Arctic, with its five tunnels, tram and 10-stamp mill penetrated North Star in the cliffs above the lower Blue Lake. Still working as late as 1936, the Arctic ranked as "a big gold producer". Just west of the Arctic stood the Ling Mine. The Senator Mine worked North Star about one-half mile east of the Arctic. As you leave, scan North Star's curving flank for tramway structures clinging to ancient pre-Cambrian rock.

Below the lakes, the Monte Cristo spreads across Quandary's south slope. R. Widmar, in his 1905 pamphlet "Blue River Gold Fields and Metal Mines", described the Monte Cristo's "six or seven foot blanket vein". A blanket ore deposit runs horizontally, sometimes just below grass roots. At the rich Monte Cristo, a generous Mother Nature had exposed the vein, revealing its zinc, lead, gold, silver, iron and copper riches. Constructed in 1904, a modern ore mill built at the Monte Cristo featured a crusher, sizing screens, concentrators and Wilfley shaker tables, impressive machinery installed by the Quandary Mining and Milling Company. An old wagon road leading to the Monte Cristo Mine takes off north just east of the county road's junction with the Wheeler National Recreation Trail. The Monte Cristo mill was across the main road on the south side. Look for the historic Senator Mine's tipsy mine tipple in the lower gulch as well.

Raw exciting views make this quick hike rewarding. High elevation limits the Blue Lakes hiking season. We hiked it three times, all in several inches of snow! Hikers also use this route to cross the saddle on Fletcher Mountain into McCullough and to climb Fletcher.

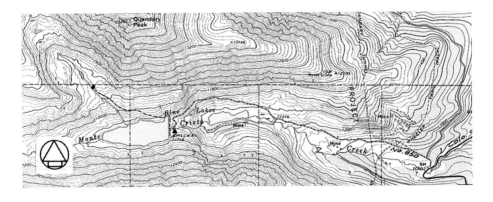

Upper Blue Lake provides a sparkling setting to begin a short hike to the Golden Beaver Mine and its historic neighbors.

In the beginning, God created the heavens and the earth. Gen. 1.1

17

2 QUANDARY PEAK

Time: 7-8 hours
Distance: 3 miles
Elevation gain: 3,145 feet
High point: 14,265 feet
Rating: Most difficult
Usually open: July-Sept.
Topo: USGS Breckenridge 1970, rev. 1987

Quandary Peak, known as one of Colorado's easiest Fourteeners, provides the neck-swiveling vistas typical of Colorado's highest mountains--but at a bargain price. The climb is tough, but it's short for a Fourteener. Panoramic views deliver a nice bonus.

Drive 7.9 miles from Breckenridge's Main Street-Park Avenue stoplight south on Colorado 9 toward Hoosier Pass. At Blue Lakes Road (No. 850), turn right, then turn right again onto No. 851. Continue 1.1 miles to the unmarked trailhead. (Avoid the double-track at 1.0 mile.) Park parallel on the logging road.

A suggestion: Stop enroute Hwy. 9 near the Quandary Peak sign and study Quandary's outline. A good idea of its contours helps hikers enjoy this outstanding climb.

Most maps recommend another trailhead, located in Monte Cristo Gulch, 0.4 miles in on No. 850. After hiking both, we suggest this book's easier route. If you use the old trail, generally keep north-northwest at the several forks. Hiking boots are important for climbing Quandary, especially on the more difficult old trail.

The trail ascends in a westerly direction. After about 10 minutes of moderate walking, follow the fork right (north) another 10 minutes or so to a trail junction. (This occurs just when you see the trees open up ahead over McCullough Gulch.) Go left, avoiding a road which looks like a ditch heading uphill.

Almost immediately, views open north to Mt. Helen and snatches of your goal, Quandary Peak. Later, a clear view of Quandary emerges. Don't be fooled by the rounded "summit". The real high point hides beyond.

At a point just below timberline meet the trail from Monte Cristo Gulch. Note this fork, almost hidden in the willows, to choose the correct route on your return. Emerge from the trees to confront a huge ridge that runs up Quandary's spine. This ridge will be your route.

Get ready for a long, steep haul. There's one breather--a short walk over level ground--before the final ascent. Then the trail will labor its way through talus, sometimes disappearing. Don't worry--the ridge remains a clear line to the top and the trail reappears.

All along the way, hikers enjoy sweeping views of Hoosier Pass and Mt. Silverheels. Directly south rise Lincoln, Bross and Democrat, three more Fourteeners that hikers can conquer in a single demanding day hike. Northeast and north lie the Blue River valley, Breckenridge and a long stretch north along the Gore Range. Across the miles note majestic Grays and Torreys Peaks, marking the Continental Divide.

Even when the day is calm in the valley, blockbuster winds may blast Quandary hikers. A wind-resistant hooded jacket that battens down nicely should be in your pack. Start early to avoid afternoon electrical storms, especially in July and August. Plan to be off the exposed tundra shortly after noon. In September, bring warm clothes.

Large rock shelters atop Quandary provide a nice resting place. Savor the views to Notch Mountain, a clefted peak west in the Saguache Range and, just beyond it, the Mount of the Holy Cross. Peer down into lake-strewn McCullough Gulch north and across to the Ten Mile Range. Tranquil South Park stretches southeast.

Quandary, named because its strange ore puzzled prospectors, lay in the Pollack Mining District established in September, 1861. The mining registry book, signed by Joseph Pollack, district recorder, has a bullet hole through its cover and pages. Legend whispers of an early day Quandary City, with a hotel and ore smelter on site, and also a camp named

Pollack with a mine and mill.

Ski touring/Snow shoeing: *(Easy)* This tour arcs through the Bemrose Ski Circus near Quandary. Park 8.7 miles south from the Main Street-Park Avenue light at Road No. 670. Check the trail sign and a *Trails Illustrated* Breckenridge map for route options. Drive a second car to Hoosier Pass. The trail begins on the summit's east side, heading north into forest. Ski 4.8 mile trip to your parked car. (You may have to walk the last section.)

Above: Hiker advances on Quandary summit. Left: Study Quandary's unusual contours before the climb. The perspective will help when you get up high.

3 McCULLOUGH GULCH

Time: 3 hours
Distance: 1.3 miles
Elevation gain: 800 feet
High point: 11,900 feet
Rating: Moderate
Usually open: July-mid-Sept.
Topo: USGS Breckenridge 1970, rev. 1987

After nearly thirty years in Colorado's majestic mountains, accepting spectacular scenery as daily fare, we still stood in wonder at the hidden glory of God's creation high in McCullough Gulch. Rich evergreens, fortresses of outcropping granite, tortuous terrain of rock and rill, gorges gleaming with the spray of icy waterfalls, green-green meadows and fragile wildflowers all combine here in a feast of nature's beauty.

Drive 7.9 miles from Breckenridge's Main Street-Park Avenue stoplight south on Colorado 9 toward Hoosier Pass (named by homesick Indiana prospectors in 1860). Turn right on County Road 850, then turn right again onto County Road 851, which takes you 2 miles into McCullough Gulch. At about 1 mile, look for the upper waterfalls, your destination. At 2 miles, park near the water diversion structures. Parking can be tricky on a busy day. The Quandary Tunnel, cutting across McCullough and Monte Cristo Gulches, supplies water to Colorado Springs on the eastern slope, with storage just over Hoosier Pass at Montgomery Reservoir, which submerges an 1860s gold rush townsite.

A beautiful falls rushes through a chasm near your parking area. Squeeze past the gate, cross a bridge and trek up the old mine road passing a lake cabin enroute. Don't miss peering into the canyon occasionally to glimpse the roaring creek below. The trailhead, a 15-minute walk, is just left of a sign marked "Private Road-No Admittance".

The trail climbs into the trees. Almost immediately note a mine tailings dump alongside a log building smashed by a massive fallen tree trunk. This unknown mine has square nails in its rotting timbers, indicating pre-1900 construction. The rock evidences blasting.

Listen to both murmur and roar as you cross rippling streams nearing the thunderous waterfalls. The trail splits below the falls, one branch leading to a lower deluge and the other to a series of falls and alpine tarns. Before this fork, you cross a creek, then have to step over a large fallen log. Please make every effort to stay on the trail.

Just 45 minutes or less of pick-your-way walking (1.2 miles) brings you to a series of eight or so gushing cascades which stair-step down from a glacial lake. A broad, limpid watercourse across smooth rock alternates with a torrent, percolating bubbly white water from a narrow chute. Striated, mottled, dappled and lichen-speckled, the rock here displays markings of gold, salmon and rust.

Despite the trail's shortness, upper McCullough Gulch offers ample opportunity for exploring around the lake at 1.3 miles and small lakes beyond. (Stay left a ways beyond the big lake and go through the rocky gap southwest.) Spend some time investigating the alpine life zone amid ancient pre-Cambrian rock formed 600 million years ago.

Quandary Mountain, at 14,265 feet Colorado's 15th highest peak, on the south and towering 13,950-foot Pacific Peak, on the north, guard McCullough Gulch. At McCullough's head, early prospector George W. Crow discovered the Alsatian Lode, which produced 150 ounces of silver and nearly an ounce of gold per tone of ore. The Northern Star high in McCullough; plus the big Governor Mine, with its mill at the southern base of the gulch just west of the Blue River; and the Quandary Queen, located on Quandary's east slope number among McCullough's mines. Miners, who found themselves "in a quandary" about the mysterious ore uncovered here, named Quandary. Molybdenum, the ore abundant on Bartlett Mountain just southwest, and also found in Quandary's salamander claims, may be the puzzling ore that prompted the name.

Ski touring/Snow shoeing: *(Moderate)* McCullough Gulch offers superb ski and snow shoe touring. You can begin at Road 851 and ski unplowed roadway into the gulch. Or, use the more demanding route from the new trailhead about 7 miles from Breckenridge on Colorado 9. Park at the small lot there. Then climb the old road. At 0.7 miles keep high on a right fork, as a left fork drops toward the creekbed. Ski to 1.5 miles at the County Road 851 junction and take that to Monte Cristo Gulch, or return on your ski tracks.

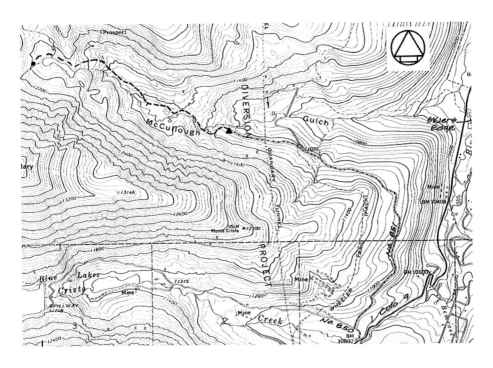

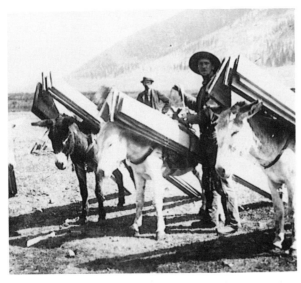

Prospector pack trains first beat paths that Breckenridge area hikers use today.

4 WHEELER NATIONAL RECREATION TRAIL

Time: 6-7 hours
Distance: 10 miles
Elevation gain: 2,250 feet
High point: 12,490 feet
Rating: More difficult
Usually open: July-mid-Sept.
Topo: USGS Breckenridge 1970, rev. 1987
USGS Copper Mt. 1970, rev. 1987

Take a walk on top of the world, with views to successive mountain ranges that look like whitecaps frozen into an arctic ocean, on the historic Wheeler National Recreation Trail. You hike from McCullough Gulch south of Breckenridge to Copper Mountain along old Judge Wheeler's sheep trail. Fifty percent of the route lies above timberline.

Two cars are required for this hike. Leave one car at trail's end near Copper Mountain: Drive west on I-70 to Copper Mountain exit 195. Cross the bridge over the interstate and immediately turn left into the Vail Pass-Ten Mile Canyon bikeway parking area.

Drive a second car to Breckenridge. Then take Colorado 9 south from the Main Street-Park Avenue stoplight 7.5 miles. Turn right onto County Road 850, then right again on Road 851 to McCullough Gulch. After you enter the gulch and begin to climb it going west, the road forks. Go right and cross the gulch to its north slope. The Wheeler Trail intersects the road just right of a sharp left turn at just under 2 miles from Road 851's beginning.

Plan to carry water and wear sturdy boots for a shard rock trail above timberline.

The trail begins at 11,100 feet, near the Little Fool Mine, and crosses a ridge to a steep drop through a burn area into the Spruce Creek valley (10,940 feet). View Continental Falls here. Cross the creek and climb to the Spruce Creek Road at 11,000 feet. Follow the aqueduct for 200 yards, watching for the trail to re-enter the woods. Navigate Crystal Creek and cross the 4WD road. The major climb on this route ascends to 12,400 feet as you mount Peak 10 on switchbacks along Crystal ridge. Views of the Crystal Creek drainage, Ten Mile Range and Blue Valley north to Silverthorne emerge. Now enjoy 1.7 miles of walking alpine tundra with only cairns to mark the trail. Look for "belly flowers", the miniature arctic zone blossoms that you must lie down on your belly to see. Cross a shallow basin between Peaks 10 and 9 and the 4WD road from Breckenridge. A road here leads to a communications facility and the historic Briar Rose Mine.

Passing over the range on a saddle between Peaks 8 and 9, impressive views of the Ten Mile, Gore, Saguache and Flat Tops Ranges unfold. Miners discovered strange metal here in the early days, recognized today as molybdenum.

As you hike above timberline, look for examples of the solifluction phenomenon in the rocks. Typical of the arctic zone and common in Alaska, this freeze-thaw process creates rock patterns in interesting shapes--polygons, cirques, garlands and streams of rock. Also check for miners' "glory holes" from the 1880s and 90s.

Be wary of the inhospitable nature of this unprotected alpine zone. Crossing snowfields on a steep pitch can trigger slides. Electrical storms present extreme danger. We hiked this trail in a September drizzle which changed into a lightning storm above treeline and heightened into an icy blizzard that obscured all signs of a trail. We wish you a better day!

The trail drops steeply to Copper Mountain. Just after crossing a creek, the Miners Creek Trail to Frisco (No. 22) heads off to the right. Great views of the upper Ten Mile Canyon, especially during autumn's aspen show, refresh you during these last two miles from the Miners Creek fork to trail's end. In the Ten Mile Canyon, follow the gas line path northerly 0.25 miles to your parked car.

The scenic Wheeler route has earned National Recreation Trail status. The track began in the 1870s when rancher Judge John Wheeler moved sheep across the Ten Mile Range to Wheeler Flats, site of today's Copper Mountain resort. Miners walked the path to Breckenridge. The trail, rebuilt in 1932, again made the high meadows a pastureland from the 1930s to 1950s. When World's Championship Pack Burro Race organizers chose this path in 1969, the trail regained hiker use.

You can make this trek in reverse, from Copper to the upper Blue beyond Breckenridge. This alternative, rated "most difficult", includes a 2,720-foot elevation gain in 3.4 miles. Exit at McCullough Gulch or choose Crystal (1.2 miles down to trailhead here), Spruce Creek (1.3 miles) or Monte Cristo Gulch (0.4 miles) to leave the trail.

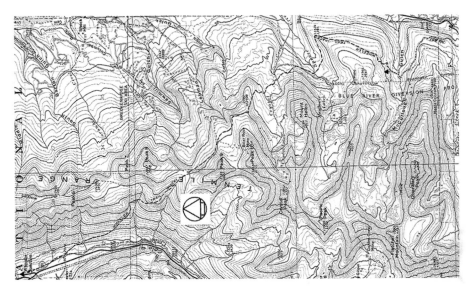

An aging ore tram structure stands against the Continental Divide's backdrop, on a short Spruce Creek side trip from the scenic Wheeler Trail. Try off-trail jaunts up Spruce, Crystal Creeks and to Briar Rose Mine.

5 MOHAWK LAKES

Time: 2-3 hours
Distance: 1.2 miles or 2.8 miles
Elevation gain: 1,000 feet, upper trail
High point: 12,100 feet
Rating: Moderate
Usually open: July-mid-Sept.
Topo: USGS Breckenridge 1970, rev. 1987

Stunning scenery, historic mine ruins and a short hike suitable for school-age kids or visiting relatives make the Mohawk Lakes Trail a favorite with locals.

Drive south 2.4 miles on Colorado 9 from Breckenridge's Main Street-Park Avenue stoplight. Turn right at the Spruce Creek Road (No. 800), just past Goose Pasture Tarn, the lake on your left. Jog left after 0.1 mile. You can choose between two trailheads for Mohawk Lakes. The lower trailhead, 1.2 miles from Colorado 9, offers a hike of 2.8 miles to the upper lake, with a 1,700-foot elevation gain. The upper trailhead, 2.7 miles from Colorado 9, requires a 4WD and may be *very* rough. But it shortens the hike to 1.2 miles. Follow the Spruce Creek Road through the Crown subdivision (the old Crown Placers) to the Arapaho National Forest Spruce Creek Portal at 10,400 feet. Park and hike along sections of an early logging road, with old flumes and a late 1880s mill structure, to join the trail. Or continue 1.5 miles to the 4WD parking area.

The upper trail climbs from 11,100 feet altitude through charming alpine landscape 0.4 miles to the Mayflower Lakes, set against a sheer mountain backdrop. Mount Helen, 13,164 feet, rises to the north. Eight log buildings and a bunkhouse stand near the lake. The Mayflower Mine, discovered August 1, 1887, ranked as a notable shipper of high grade ore in 1888. Miners "lost" the gold-bearing vein, so the mine stood idle for years until a new 200-foot tunnel struck the main vein, yielding ore rich as 30 ounces of gold per ton.

Tom Davidson, a hermit, lived alone in this deserted camp in the early 1900s, according to author Perry Eberhart. He was discovered dead in his cabin around 1920 and his sole companion, a loyal cat, was found frozen stiff on a windowsill.

Continuing beyond Mayflower to Mohawk Lakes, investigate the old mill set on a dramatic view location. Note the massive wooden machinery supports, a hefty 5x5x2 feet, constructed from layered strips of cut lumber. A large wheel, used to generate water power, lies nearby. Brick from a smelter is scattered about. Owners of a private cabin here ask your respect but allow use of the building as a storm shelter.

Note a thick aerial cable which connects to a tramway structure above. And don't miss Continental Falls, tumbling through three chasms above and north of the mill.

The trail curves and climbs to the lower Mohawk Lake, first called Foster Lake, below massive 13,950-foot Pacific Peak. Follow a trail near a tumbling stream from this lake's south side to find upper Mohawk. The Forest Service requests that you walk on rocks through the fragile alpine tundra to protect vulnerable plant life here.

Evidence of mining abounds. Ore bearing fissure veins in the Ten Mile Range provided silver and gold ore for companies like the Glen-Mohawk-Mt. Gilead Mining Company, whose tunnel here extended 816 feet in 1905. The Garrison and Black Prince Mines also operated nearby. Miners fared well in these arctic life zone level mines despite extreme temperatures because their tunnels averaged 55 degrees year round.

Ski touring/Snow shoeing: *(Moderate)* Drive No. 800 to the end of the plowed road. Glide southwest, staying on Spruce Creek Road. Forest breaks afford views first of Pacific Peak, west-southwest, then Quandary. At 0.3 miles, note a switchback and turnoff for the Burro Trail through Carter gulch and down Lehman to Peak 9's base.

A slight drop at 0.6 miles and a southwest bend precede a climb to more open terrain. At 1.2 miles meet the steep Crystal Creek aqueduct road with its green gate. You continue left past this road and reach the Wheeler Trail junction at 1.9 miles. From here, continue straight on the upper road. At the clearing, a potential avalanche area, drop down to the creek below and regain the road on the north side of Spruce Creek. Continue another 0.6 miles to the aqueduct and views of Mt. Helen and the rugged Ten Mile Range. Watch the return trip for fast snow conditions--pole drag or ski side road powder to control speed.

Another tour climbs the lower trail to intersect the road, then a roadway schuss down.

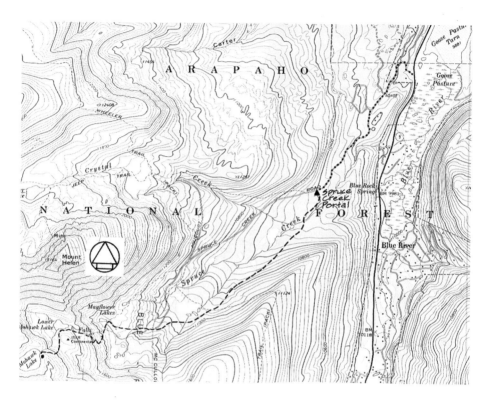

A massive ore mill commands a Continental Divide view from the history-rich Mohawk Lakes Trail.

6 CRYSTAL LAKES

Time: 3-4 hours
Distance: 2 miles
Elevation gain: 1,000 feet (lower lake)
High point: 11,980 feet (lower lake)
Rating: More difficult
Usually open: July-mid-Sept.
Topo: USGS Breckenridge 1970, rev. 1987

Unsurpassed views, first of the mineral-rich mountains in Breckenridge's gold-latticed "back yard", then of the craggy Continental Divide peaks, reward the hiker who makes the hard, short climb to the Crystal Lakes. Two alpine tarns above timberline, set in the ancient, glacier-carved rock of this rugged section of towering Ten Mile Range mountains, glisten like jewels in a rough, rock-hewn setting. This hike goes to lower Crystal Lake.

Drive 2.4 miles south on Colorado 9 from Breckenridge's Main Street-Park Avenue stoplight. Turn right at the Spruce Creek Road (No. 800), just past Goose Pasture Tarn, the lake on your left. Jog left after 0.1 mile. Proceed 1.2 miles to the Arapaho National Forest Spruce Creek Portal. Park here and walk up the road 0.25 miles to the trailhead sign: "Lower Crystal Lake: 2 miles". The road has a green gate.

(One alternate route cuts elevation gain by 600 feet. Drive the Spruce Creek-Mohawk Lakes 4WD road to its junction with the Wheeler Trail. Park and walk the Wheeler Trail northwest to the Crystal road. Go left. Or, drive the Crystal Road to its creekside closure.)

The trail starts at the green gate on the right and begins a stiff climb on an 1880s wagon road now used by 4WD vehicles. When you pause to catch your breath and a jeep bounces by, you may want to hitch a ride. But the walker's way to Crystal Lake rewards the determined with the cool breath of a spruce forest, unfolding views of panoramic stretches of mountains and a garden of wildflowers--all joys sacrificed by four-wheelers.

The road ascends through scented spruce beside rushing Crystal Creek. At 1.2 miles, cross the Wheeler National Recreation Trail. Look for a waterfall enroute and views of Bald Mountain, dome-shaped Barney Ford Hill, the old narrow gauge railway route over Ford Hill, then up Boreas Pass and the Indiana Creek valley, where early stagecoaches ran. Bathed in splashes of autumn's golden brilliance, this view seemed beautiful, but it proved only a teaser for staggering vistas to come.

We reached the lower lake in one hour and 45 minutes of slow climbing, with many photo stops. Three fishermen passed us at a good clip. They had already disappeared behind the ridge from the visible trail across talus on Peak 10 enroute to the upper lake when we arrived at the lower. This 1.9-mile upper lake trail crosses the south slope of Peak 10 to the right (north), switchbacks, then heads southwest to the upper lake, which is located at 12,850 feet, due west of the lower. The high lake is surrounded by mines and shadowed by 13,852-foot Crystal Peak.

Half an old log cabin remains at the lower lake. A mine road leading toward 13,164-foot Mt. Helen on the left (south) once served several lode mines. The lead-based ores here yielded silver. Mt. Helen silver claims shipped 100 sacks of good grade ore to the Leadville smelter in October, 1936, according to a news clip. On Peak 10, the famous Briar Rose Mine produced prodigious amounts of silver.

The *Rocky Mountain News*, in a September, 1883 article on Summit County's potential, listed Crystal Lake as one of the county's eleven bustling mine camps. In 1881, volunteers built the road to this camp in return for stock in the new toll road company. "The road can be built for $750 to Crystal Lake...", a June 7, 1881 *Breckenridge Daily Journal* reported.

That same year, Summit County produced $2.6 million in gold, silver, copper, lead and zinc. Multiply that figure by nine to obtain today's inflated value—$23.4 million. And that doesn't factor in gold's price rise from around $20 per ounce to over $300 per ounce.

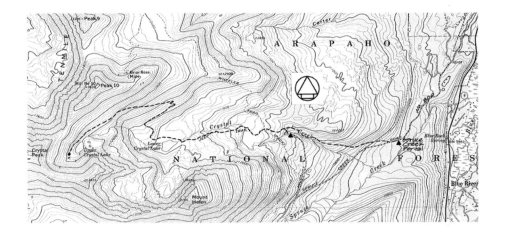

*Hiker at lower
Crystal Lake scans
mountainside for
upper trail to second
lake at 12,850 feet, a
fishermen's favorite.*

7 INDIANA CREEK

Time: 3 hours
Distance: 3.3 miles
Elevation gain: 541 feet
High point: 12,029 feet
Rating: Moderate
Usually open: July-Sept.
Topo: USGS Breckenridge 1970, rev. 1987
    USGS Boreas Pass 1994

A heavily-traveled stage route featuring a famous mine and two ghost town sites, this historic hike offers a trip backward into Summit's yesteryears. The hike begins atop the Continental Divide on 11,488-foot Boreas Pass with its sweeping views, then drops down through green, forested Indiana Gulch.

Two cars are required. Leave one car at trail's end above Spruce Valley Ranch before the hike begins: Drive 1.3 miles south on Colorado 9 from Breckenridge's Main Street-Park Avenue stoplight to the Wagon Road (No. 11). Turn left and proceed 2.7 miles, veering left twice, to park beyond the skeet shooting range. Indiana Creek Road is a public access.

Drive Colorado 9 with the second car, north toward Breckenridge. At the light turn right on Boreas Pass Road (No. 10) and proceed 9.6 miles to the Boreas summit. The road, built on the Denver South Park & Pacific's narrow-gauge rail roadbed, climbs gold-rich Barney Ford Hill, passes Breckenridge's old-time picnic spot, Rocky Point, and climbs to 100-year old Bakers Tank, which replenished thirsty railway steam engines. Beautiful views emerge, to (l. to r.) Mount Helen, Pacific Peak, Crystal Peak and Peak 10, with Goose Pasture Tarn below. At the Boreas summit, a depot, roundhouse, section house and the nation's highest U.S. postoffice once straddled the Continental Divide. Park at the summit.

The trail rises smartly on the only climb on this hike. Hoosier Ridge stretches along the Divide from Boreas Pass to Hoosier Pass. A short (0.5 mile) but hard climb up the jeep road west (right) takes you up Hoosier Ridge. Then drop down from the high point to a saddle. Note the mine shaft here with its 1880s square nails. Now descend north into the Indiana Creek drainage. Soon look for a mine shaft building high on your left and a cabin on the trail. Continue down to a very old log cabin in heavy pines.

Notice tailings at 1.4 miles as you approach the site of the big Warriors Mark Mine on your right. Discovered in 1879 by Colorado's famous "Snowshoe Itinerant", Methodist minister John Lewis Dyer, this rich silver mine stands at 11,095 feet altitude. Extensive tailings from open pit mining, equipment, shaft holes and a large concentrating mill in ruins will interest mining buffs.

Just 0.3 miles beyond the Warriors Mark lies the Dyersville ghost camp, named after the skiing preacher who built the first cabin here in 1881. Today four log buildings remain at Dyersville, with a fifth just down the road. A big grassy meadow soon opens up. Look for two sets of tailings overgrown by evergreens on the south side, as well as three ruined buildings here. A sign indicates the road to Pennsylvania Creek. Ford the stream and continue the last 0.3 miles along the old stagecoach route. This early route began as a toll road authorized by the Colorado Territorial Legislature and built in 1861. The Spottswood & McClellan Stage Line made the 18-mile Boreas trip from Como to Breckenridge six times weekly in up-to-date Concord coaches on this road.

Driving out you will pass the century-old site of Conger's Camp, once located in a horseshoe-shaped meadow near the Indiana Creek Road-Argentine Drive intersection. Before 1882, Spottswood & McClellan stagecoaches had delivered mail and passengers here. Conger's sprang up below the rich Diantha silver lode, a "blanket" vein discovered by Colonel Samuel P. Conger on the south hillside at about 10,450 feet. A Civil War colonel, Indian scout and locator of the rich Caribou mine near Nederland, Conger launched his town with a postoffice, sawmill, ore mill, stores and 30-40 houses.

Ski touring: *(Easy)* Travel 3.4 miles up Boreas Pass Road to the plowed skier's parking area. The old railway roadbed provides a gentle 2.8 percent grade for a glorious sunny day tour. (Old Boreas, god of the wind, can scour this route with icy breath on cold days.) Enjoy spectacular mountain views starting at 0.4 miles. Enter the trees at about 1.0 miles, then at 1.4 miles, cross the open basin, formerly a rail stop for Conger's below. Bakers Tank at 3.4 miles makes a good stop, but strong skiers can go to the summit (7.1 miles).

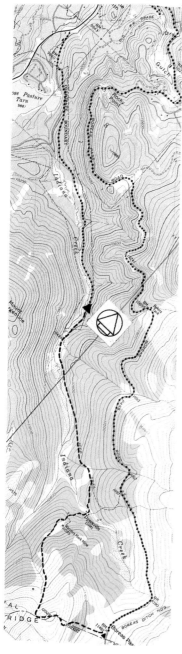

Begin at historic Boreas Pass summit for Indiana Creek tour. Highest U.S. post office straddled the Continental Divide at 1880 rail station here.

Century-old Bakers Tank stands newly-restored on Boreas Pass Road.

8 BLACK POWDER PASS

Time: 2-3 hours
Distance: 1.7 mile
Elevation gain: 671 feet
High point: 12,159 feet
Rating: Moderate
Usually open: July-Aug.
Topo: USGS Boreas Pass 1994

Follow the old Denver, South Park & Pacific narrow gauge rail route (now a roadway) to a trailhead at the Boreas Pass summit for this historic hike. The railway's old log section house atop Boreas stands as a reminder of smoke-and-cinder days gone by. Echoes of train whistles and chugging locomotives still float on the Boreas Pass breeze.

Bring a topo map for this hike because the trail is not well defined.

Drive Colorado 9 south from Breckenridge's Main Street-Park Avenue stoplight 0.2 miles to Boreas Pass Road (No. 10). Proceed 9.6 miles to the summit. Along the route you may wish to detour at 1.2 miles to see the Washington Mine on Rd. No. 518 into Illinois Gulch. An old shaft house, mine railway, dynamite shack and artifacts remain to intrigue visitors. Contact the Summit Historical Society for a mine tour here.

Continue the drive past many silver mines to century-old Bakers Tank at 6.6 miles. It slaked the thirst of hard-working steam locomotives. Proceed past open upper meadows at 8.4 miles and beyond where Baldy, Lincoln, Hoosier Ridge, Silverheels and Pacific Peaks offer superb vistas. The 7:40 Mine operated at the old town of Farnham here. At the summit, note stone ruins at right where an 1884 stone engine house with a rail turntable once stood. (See Gilliland's history *SUMMIT* for the full story of the old railway. For a mile by mile tour of the historic Boreas Pass road, take along Gilliland's ghost town guide, *BRECKENRIDGE!*)

The trail begins near the recently-restored section house. Walk northeast from this building along the dirt track labeled "Boreas Ditch No. 2" on the topo map. The hike's goal is a saddle between Boreas Mountain (south) and Bald Mountain (north). The route follows a stream drainage to its destination at 12,159 feet.

The track cuts through a meadow strewn with stumps from old timber cuts. Miners and railroaders often denuded an area of its trees for construction and firewood. Soon the trail hugs a forested slope on the stream's right side. Later the trail crosses the watercourse climbing above treeline to the pass summit. Be prepared to lose the trail at times. Just follow the drainage on up.

Wildflowers make this trail a delight. Many varied species grow near the old rail station site. Above, look for orange, red and fuchsia Indian paintbrush in vivid clumps. In the meadows above treeline thick masses of flowers bloom streamside. At the summit, a myriad of tiny alpine cushion flowers will please those willing to stop and see their beauty.

At top, views sweep down to South Park. Across to the north lies historic French Pass where 1870s stagecoaches created a lively transportation scene. As late as 1899, following the Winter of the Big Snow, stagecoach excursions visited French Pass for passengers to marvel at the deep July snowdrifts. Record snows that year buried the rail station, with only a curl of smoke above the section house to evidence life there. Snow shut down the railroad for 79 days.

Hardy hikers can extend this short trek by climbing another 1,000 feet to the 13,082-foot Boreas Mountain summit or 13,684-foot Baldy. Baldy is a 1,500-foot trek with several false summits enroute.

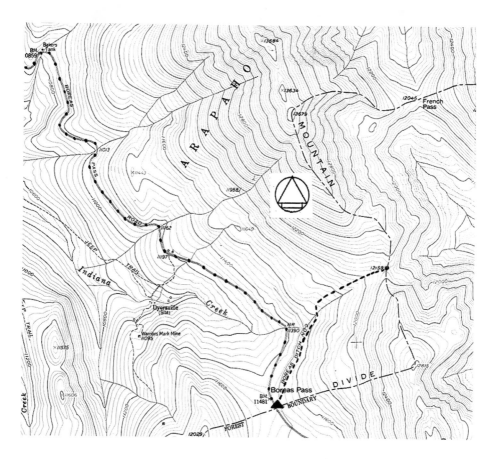

Parry's primrose (left) and moss colony (right) are trailside pleasures.

31

9 PEAKS TRAIL

Time: 5 hours
Distance: 10 miles
Elevation gain: 200 feet
High point: 10,200 feet
Rating: More difficult
Usually open: Mid-June-Sept.
Topo: Trails Illustrated Breckenridge South and Vail-Frisco-Dillon

On a hot day, hike this cool, shaded trail through a flower-decked pine forest all the way from Breckenridge to Frisco. Forest freshness, the icy splash of eight major creeks to cross and a consistent altitude of just over 10,000 feet will refresh and invigorate hikers.

Two cars are required for this hike. Leave one car in Frisco at the bikeway parking lot on West Main Street, just 0.1 miles east of I-70 exit 201.

Drive a second car on Colorado 9 to Ski Hill Road in Breckenridge. Turn west at the stop light there and proceed past the Peak 8 ski area to the signed trailhead, 2.2 miles.

The trail, a clear path through dense forest, cuts north across the lower flanks of Ten Mile Range, crossing Peaks 7 to 1, ending at Frisco. At the beginning, follow an irrigation ditch, and later encounter a small lake. Here, take the downhill trail to the right, not the upper with its red diamond mark. Generally, the Peaks Trail is very well marked with blue diamonds. This fork is the only point of confusion.

The man-made lake here, part of an idyllic turn-of-the-century summer resort developed by Colonel Lemuel "Nuggets" Kingsbury, was stocked with trout in 1904 in preparation for the debut of his Iowa Hill Resort on "Banner Lake".

The creeks, spanned by log bridges, are beautiful Cucumber (named for a prospector in Breckenridge's 1859 gold rush discovery party), and later South, Middle and North Barton, with a couple of unnamed extras thrown in (see map). The trail becomes muddy near the creeks during rainy periods. Insect repellent comes in handy for these areas.

Fields of lavender-blue lupine colored the July forest floor on the Breckenridge section of the trail, with Indian paintbrush and monkshood in the shady woods as well. Near Frisco, find a garden of wildflowers, with blue columbine, the Colorado state flower, wild rose and harebell.

Signs along the trail inform hikers of mileage. At the Peaks, Miners Creek and Gold Hill Trail junction, a sign indicates your progress of six miles from Breckenridge to this point.

A profusion of aspen, pine and willow, alive with rushing streams and beaver ponds on rolling terrain, makes the area below Peaks 2 and 3 a delight. Pretty, open meadows, some with wild strawberries, offer more views as the trail drops approaching Frisco.

Watch carefully for blue diamonds as you cross the 4WD roads in the Rainbow Lake area. The trail will lead past an old ski jump near Bill's Ranch (Bill Thomas' family owned an 1870s Frisco hotel). Then the trail connects to the paved bikepath leading to the bikeway parking area.

The Peaks Trail, built by the U.S. Forest Service with local volunteers and later improved by Colorado Mountain Club and Colorado Outdoor Education Center members, does not appear on the USGS maps. The trail generally follows the 10,200-foot contour lines to the Gold Hill junction on the map recommended above, then drops to Rainbow Lake parallel to the 4WD road. Be aware: This trail is popular with mountain bikers.

Ski touring: *(More difficult)* Skiers driving to the trail may choose to pick up the path at its Ski Hill Road access to avoid removing skis at the plowed road crossing. Skiers using the free Summit Stage bus line can pick up the trail near the Peak 8 ski area: Walk to the upper parking lot, north of the ski area restaurants. The trail begins at the rear of the lot and quickly joins the official Peaks Trail. Look for a red diamond here.

Three steep drops, at Cucumber, South Barton and Middle Barton Creeks, add advanced challenge to this wooded trail. However, we skied it with novices who had no real difficulty because each had mastered a strong snowplow. You can begin the tour at Frisco, but you will face a stiff climb. Begin at Breckenridge to enjoy descending terrain.

The Summit Stage bus line provides skiers a free lift back to Breckenridge.

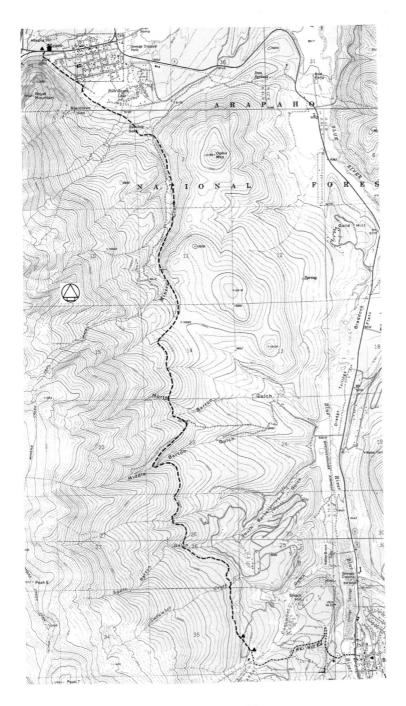

10 THE MAIL RUN

Time: 6-7 hours
Distance: 6.4 miles
Elevation gain: 1,760 feet
High point: 12,300 feet
Rating: More difficult
Usually open: July-Sept.
Topo: Trails Illustrated Idaho Springs Georgetown Loveland Pass

Two intriguing ghost towns, a silver mine camp and a funky half-ghost town make the early day Mail Run route an historic hike.

Two cars are required. Leave the first car in Montezuma at the Sts. John Road parking area. To get there drive U.S. 6 to Keystone. Turn onto the Montezuma Road (No. 5) east of Keystone Lodge and continue 5.6 miles to the Sts. John Road at right.

Drive a second vehicle on Colorado 9 to the Tiger Road (No. 6), 3.5 miles north of Breckenridge. Set your odometer here. Proceed east on the Tiger Road to the fork at 5.7 miles. Veer left for the North Fork of the Swan River and old Rexford. Pass a road at 6.4 miles and one of several gates at 6.5 miles and a road at 6.6 miles. At 6.7 miles take the timber road left uphill. At 7.6 miles reach the old Rexford Road. Park here.

For a mile-by-mile history of the gold-rich Tiger Road and its many mines and communities, use Mary Ellen Gilliland's ghost town guide, *BRECKENRIDGE!*

The trail follows a rough wagon road to the Rexford ghost town, where ruins of a general store, assay office, saloon, boardinghouse, postoffice and Rochester Queen mine office remain in a grassy meadow. (See Gilliland's gold rush history, *SUMMIT,* for details.)

Continue on the road past Rexford to a point where the road forms a major hairpin curve to the right. This is where you leave the road. Note the stream at left in the valley rising northwest. This drainage leads to a pass at 12,300 feet, your next destination. The pass lies just west of the Glacier Mountain point marked on the topo as 12,384 feet. Note: Jeepers have torn up this previously untouched valley. Avoid following their unauthorized road when it veers east up the valley. Your route goes north.

This lush valley, cut by an icy stream, provides an idyllic hiking experience. Keep an eye on the stream till you see the saddle, staying right at stream forks. Use the topo map and a compass as a guide. Continue to the rocky pass.

A broad alpine bowl spreads below as you descend north from the pass. Hikers should pick a route bearing north toward the Wild Irishman mine camp. Generally, stay on the valley's right side beneath the Glacier Mountain ridge that dominates the area.

Look for the yellow monkeyflower at stream crossings. Mosses in bright lime and kelly green flourish on mid-stream islands here. The General Teller mine straddles the ridge above right at 12,400 feet.

Hikers will spy the Wild Irishman camp near timberline below. A silver camp set in a sweet green meadow, the Wild Irishman erupted into life in the late 1870s when New York policeman Michael Dulhaney cried "Eureka". Legend says his shriek backed up the creek and washed away three silver camps! The free spirited Dulhaney always wore a battered policeman's hat.

Follow the road downhill to remains of the prim silver camp of Sts. John where the state's first silver strike took place in 1863. Unlike its Colorado cousins, Sts. John had no bawdy saloons but offered its highbrow residents a 350-volume library. Sinners had to travel to Montezuma for a spree.

Ski touring/Snow shoeing: *(Moderate)* Use the Montezuma trailhead for a ski trip up the Sts. John Road to the Wild Irishman. Drive to Montezuma using the directions above.

Follow the trail to Sts. John, keeping right at the first fork at 0.5 miles which leads to the Mark Twain and St. Elmo Mines. Continue past Sts. John. You reach the timberline camp at 3.0 miles. Check avalanche conditions before you go. Chutes at Sts. John and beyond present hazard. Try to go after a fresh snowfall because a tour operator has in recent years run a snocat over the trail without using a groomer.

Hiker indicates route for group seeking Mail Run trail.

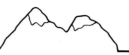
11 TEN MILE MEADOWS

Via Peaks Trail
Time: 5-6 hours
Distance: 5 miles
Elevation gain: 2,300 feet
Rating: Most difficult
High point: 11,400 feet
Usually open: July-Sept.
Topo: USGS Frisco 1970, rev. 1987

Via upper trailhead
Time: 2-3 hours
Distance: 2 miles
Elevation gain: 1,450 feet
Rating: More difficult

A picnicker's paradise awaits hikers in a high meadow below sheer, dramatic Peak 3 where a stream runs and wildflowers blossom. A trail, well-groomed by the Forest Service, gets you there on a long or short hike, depending on your choice of trailhead.

Via Peaks Trail: (5-mile hike) **Drive** I-70 to Frisco exit 201 and turn east onto Main Street. Proceed 0.1 miles to the bikeway parking lot. Enter the bikeway and go left at the intersection, walking 0.6 miles to the Peaks Trail located in a meadow near a pond. Follow the blue diamonds of the Peaks Trail for 3.0 miles to the Miners Creek junction. Watch for blue diamonds at road crossings near Rainbow Lake at 1.5 miles. Then climb through lush stream-laced woods dotted with lupine and columbine on a steady uphill trek.

Via upper trailhead: (2-mile hike--4WD required) **Drive** 0.5 miles south of the Frisco Main Street stoplight on Colorado 9. Turn right at this second stoplight and follow the blue diamonds to the Rainbow Lakes Camping Area. Miners Creek Road continues as a 4WD road from here. The road grinds along for 3.0 miles of difficult roadbed, with many confusing side roads. At the sign reading "End of road--1 mile", the road becomes very difficult. We parked at the roadside cabin near there and walked, crossing the creek just beyond and continuing straight, not left, at the junction beyond the creek. When you see a cabin ruin at right and a half cabin beyond, you have reached the early-day logging camp at the Miners Creek trailhead.

The trail begins at this early logging camp. Look for three tree trunks twisted together and spiraled in a surrealistic display. A fence here has gates for the Peaks Trail and Miners Creek Trail, your route.

The trail, nicely maintained, is blazed all the way to the meadows below 12,933-foot Tenmile Peak and 12,676-foot Peak 3 In September, hunt for mushrooms in the fallen logs. We saw buttons on a rotting trunk and orange fluted beauties on a sawn stump.

At the first of three meadows, a jagged raw-rock headwall rises starkly above a rich field studded in September with purple mountain gentian. The trail's only panoramic view unfolds here, a sweep across to the Continental Divide east, with the green-forested Blue River valley below and a long view into the Swan River valley east. The rich Swan, dredged for gold to its bedrock in the early 1900s, produced millions of dollars from gold-latticed area gulches and gold-seamed mountains from 1861 on.

A second meadow, battered by avalanches from the sheer talus-covered mountain wall above, lacks the beauty of the first. But a nice bridge here gets you across the stream.

A rock cairn marks the entrance to the third Ten Mile meadow, a flower-carpeted valley bisected by a tiny stream. Granite peaks loom above sheltering snowfields here and blossoming tundra there.

If you walk up the Miners Creek Trail another short distance, you will enjoy a view of Dillon Reservoir. Huge stumps from trees cut at snow level in winter remain. The trail scales a steep rise here to a saddle below Peak 4.

The Miners Creek Trail (No. 22) continues along the top of the Ten Mile Range between Peaks 4 and 7, marked only by cairns above timberline. The trail connects with the Wheeler Trail (No. 4), a link west to Copper Mountain and south toward Hoosier Pass.

Ski touring: *(Moderate)* The wintry Miners Creek 4WD road becomes a delightful cross-country route. The road undulates through pretty forest before climbing sharply to the roadside cabin, a good destination at 3.0 miles and a shelter in bad weather. Ski from the bikepath following blue diamonds to Rainbow Lake, then ski the Miners Creek road. Or use the second access via Colorado 9 to Miners Creek Road. Snowmobiles use the lower portion of this road.

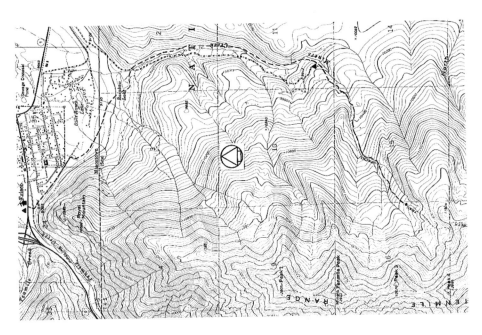

Log bridge spans stream in meadow below Peak 3. Ten Mile Meadows make a scenic stopping point on Miners Creek trail that continues on to cross rugged Ten Mile Range.

I will lift up mine eyes unto the hills, from whence cometh my help.
Ps.121:1

12 MT. VICTORIA

Time: 5 hours
Distance: 2.3 miles
Elevation gain: 2,690 feet
High point: 11,785 feet
Rating: More difficult
Usually open: July-Sept.
Topo: USGS Frisco 1970, rev. 1987

A big alpine meadow at nearly 12,000 feet gives Mt. Victoria hikers incredible Summit County views. The mountain, riddled by gold and silver seekers, echoes the past with glory holes, collapsed mine tunnels and cabin ruins enroute. A steep climb (use boots) in a short distance, the trail affords many of the enticements of its neighbor, Peak One, without the precarious rock climb to the Peak One summit.

Drive 0.1 miles east from I-70 on Frisco's Main Street to the bikepath parking area. Enter the paved bikeway trail system and veer left for the route to Breckenridge. Walk 0.5 miles to the Mt. Royal trail at right.

The trail will climb above old Masontown to pass the Mt. Royal cutoff and ascend south to the Mt. Victoria summit. Climbers use this route for Peak One also. Before you go, take a look at these three peaks from Dillon or Frisco. Note the three-tier arrangement north to south: Mt. Royal, then Victoria and the triple summits of Peak One soaring to 12,805 feet.

At the bikepath-Mt. Royal trail junction, pick up the footpath for the short climb to Masontown. (See No. 13 for Masontown's story.) At the first big tailings mound, meet a fork. Both routes go to Masontown. Go left to see ruins of 1860s-discovered Victoria Mine claims. Pass a small mine road. Then turn right onto a significant dirt road for the short jaunt to Masontown. Pass a road at left. At the clearing just before the town ruins, go left (avoid a trail marked with red diamonds) and pass through old Masontown.

Beyond the ruins the stroll turns into a trek. A great September hike because of abundant aspen forest, this trail presents a good opportunity to study the changing leaves-- especially during a pause to catch one's breath!

Experts say the aspens' brilliant gold occurs when shorter days and cooler nights deprive leaves of the green pigment called chlorophyll. As the green chlorophyll fades away, other colors--gold, orange, red--are exposed. Without chlorophyll, which uses sunlight to produce nutrients for the aspen, the leaf weakens and breaks from the tree. Then the tree will rest, its vital functions slowed to conserve energy for winter.

After leaving the aspen, you'll reach the cutoff for Mt. Royal. Keep going straight ahead here. Soon mine remains (left) and a log building (right) appear. Just beyond lies a great view spot with Buffalo Mountain's south slope, towering peaks of the Ten Mile Range and the Uneva Pass area at close range. Notice the massive size of tree trunks here.

Owners of another cabin, built to serve the adjacent mine, obviously also took advantage of the superb view. The trail crosses a rock-littered tailings mound. Here the path becomes lightly defined. It passes through an eerie rock-encrusted area amid sparse trees then emerges to an open slope where a communications facility perches atop the rise. If you've lost the path, set the building's south facing door directly behind you and proceed. You'll see the trail.

The alpine meadow and rounded tundra dome nearby is this hike's destination. Some hikers may wish to continue to conquer Peak One. This book does not recommend that trail. If you're curious about private Uneva Lake, hidden in the Ten Mile Canyon, you can spot it west from this meadow.

Enjoy views of the mountains around Breckenridge; the Swan valley; Swan Mountain; Lake Dillon; the Continental Divide; the Williams Fork Range, with Ptarmigan Mountain and Ute Peak prominent; the view past Uneva to Vail Pass; the North Ten Mile Canyon;

and Buffalo Mountain.

Returning hikers may lose the trail at timberline. Just stay atop the ridge--don't drop off either side--and you'll come off the ridge in the correct place to see the trail.

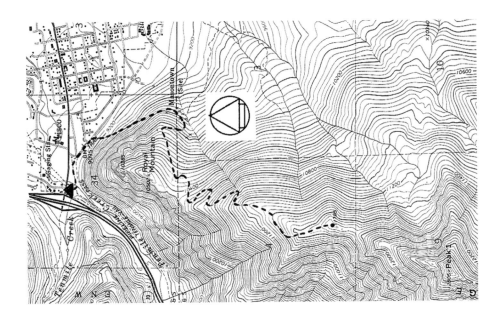

Plunging views to Lake Dillon and beyond to Continental Divide characterize Mt. Victoria trail. Right: Avalanche scar marks Victoria in three-tier mountain setting.

13 MT. ROYAL TO MASONTOWN

Time: 1-2 hours
Distance: 0.9 miles
Elevation gain: 500 feet
High point: 9,600 feet
Rating: Easy-moderate
Usually open: June-Sept.
Topo: USGS Frisco 1970, rev. 1987

Introduce youngsters ages four and up to mountain hiking on the Mt. Royal trail to old Masontown. Parents will love the Lake Dillon views and the mining history. You pass 10 lode mine tunnel sites enroute to the townsite, where ruins of a mill, bricks from a smelter and cabin foundations remain.

Drive I-70 to Frisco exit 201. Turn east onto Main Street and continue 0.1 miles to the bikeway parking area. Pick up the bikepath, going left at the fork. (Look for pasque flower in June here.) Follow this for about 0.5 miles, passing some homes on the left and boulder outcroppings on the right, to the Mt. Royal trailhead.

The trail rises diagonally across Mt. Royal's rocky foot on the right. Climbing through pretty boulder-strewn woods, the path leads to open areas with wide views of Dillon Reservoir. Workers topped the dam in 1963 and the lake stood full in 1965. Aspen mixed with verdant lodgepole pine make the forest beautiful at any time but spectacular in September. The footpath forks as you approach the Masontown site. The lower trail intersects a road leading uphill to the ghost town. The upper fork goes directly to Masontown. Choose one to go by and the second to return in order to see the evidence of mining here. Look for tailings mounds and caved-in tunnel openings. The 1866-discovered Victoria Mine had five claims--the Rosa, Golden Anne, Lebanon, Lebtoria and Victoria. The neighboring Eureka had seven. The Masontown Gold Mining & Milling Company consolidated these around 1900, built a boarding house and completed a 20-ton cyanide ore mill. In 1903, the company purchased Breckenridge's well-known Wilson smelter to move and erect at the Masontown site. Look for evidence of these old buildings at the town site. The mill remained until the 1960s when it was taken down and rebuilt at a mine in another state, according to Frisco locals.

A road at Masontown continues up, forking to lead to either the cliffs of 10,502-foot Mt. Royal (right fork) or the ridge below Peak One (left fork), both steeper climbs than the Masontown trail. (See Nos. 12 and 14.) The road also passes the avalanche path from the 1926 slide that smashed much of old Masontown to smithereens! Snow from neighboring Victoria slammed down, leaving a scar on Victoria's slope still visible here and from the highway below. Ski touring is not advised here because of the avalanche potential, and because the trail is too narrow.

(See *SUMMIT, A Gold Rush History of Summit County, Colorado* by Mary Ellen Gilliland for stories of the Masontown fiddler and the town's mysterious 1860s mine developer, General Buford.)

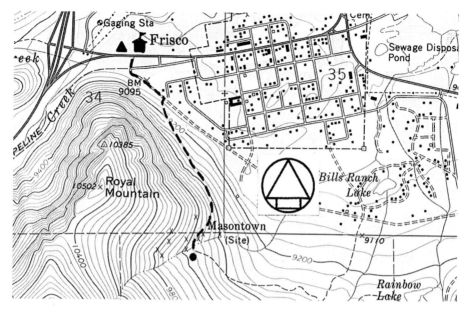

Above: Snowslide path on forested Mt. Victoria ends at old Masontown, smashed to smithereens by 1926 avalanche.

Mt. Royal's aspen-lined path, especially beautiful in autumn, makes a great trail for youngsters.

41

14 MT. ROYAL SUMMIT

Time: 2 1/2-3 hours
Distance: 1.4 miles
Elevation gain: 1,407 feet
High point: 10,502 feet
Rating: More difficult
Usually open: Mid-June-early Oct.
Topo: USGS Frisco 1970, rev. 1987

Gnarled and twisted tree limbs, with ghostly arms that reach out to entreat visitors, create an eerie fascination at Mt. Royal's summit. The trees are limber pine, one of 110 species in the pine family, and reminiscent of its long-lived cousin, the bristlecone.

Climbing Mt. Royal is a bit like going to the viewing deck of a city skyscraper. Its cliff-top summit provides drop-dead views.

Drive I-70 to Frisco exit 201 and use the directions for Mt. Victoria (No. 12).

The trail provides a huffa-puffa workout as hikers gain 800 feet altitude in the 0.4 miles beyond Masontown to the Mt. Royal trail junction. There a 90-degree right turn puts you on the short 0.1-mile path to the Mt. Royal summit.

A broad open area, encrusted with rock, provides a viewing platform. Through a dramatic cleft in the rock, note the sheer drop to the Ten Mile Canyon. "Toy" cars and trucks shoot along the tiny I-70 route 140 stories below.

The panorama takes in the five-mile deep North Ten Mile Canyon; 12,777-foot Buffalo Mountain; Lake Dillon with the Continental Divide beyond (good views of Grays and Torreys Peaks also); a sweep across 10,199-foot Ophir Mountain to the Swan River valley; Swan Mountain; and the ski runs of Keystone, North Peak and the Outback. Mt. Guyot rises starkly in the southeast.

Mt. Royal's summit offers some good picnic spots. A peeled log structure atop the knoll serves as a conversation piece and lunch spot. After lunch explore the former mining area. The footpath continues southwest for a short distance to a mine shaft hewn in solid rock.

Enroute down, spend some time at old Masontown. (See No. 13 for Masontown history and also Mary Ellen Gilliland's *SUMMIT, A Gold Rush History of Summit County, Colorado.*) Symbolic of the town's silver-studded past is a trio of thick aspens growing beside a ruined building's foundation. The trees, located beside an old cut trunk, sprang up from an aspen root that refused to die.

Echoes of Frisco's mining past linger on cool currents of mountain air. In the stillness, sounds from Frisco and busy Hwy. 9 waft up the mountainside. Certainly Masontown's early day residents heard sounds of an occasional barroom brawl in Frisco or the noisy chug-chug and warning scream of the narrow gauge locomotive arriving from Breckenridge. Each engineer had his own signature whistle, recognized by residents.

Masontown generated its own noise during heyday years. General Buford's 1866 gold-copper strike here grew to 12 active claims. Around 1905 the huge 200x300-foot stamp mill, crushing 50 ore tons daily, created a massive boom. The brick smelter clanged as workers wielding iron implements tended the furnace.

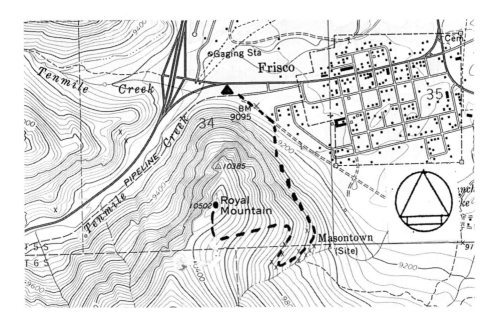

Sheer 1,400-foot drop to I-70.

Limber pine forms grotesque horse-faced figure.

15 TEN MILE CANYON NATIONAL RECREATION TRAIL

Time: 3 hours
Distance: 6 miles
Elevation gain: 600 feet
High point: 9,760 feet
Rating: Easy
Usually open: June-Sept.
Topo: USGS Frisco 1970, rev. 1987
      USGS Vail Pass 1970, rev. 1987

This paved recreation path attracts bicyclists, but also appeals to joggers and strollers. Although the trail is not a forest footpath, this book includes it because it offers easy access to the Canyon's rich railroad and silver mining history on a route level and easy to walk.

Drive I-70 to Frisco exit 201 and turn east onto Main Street. Proceed 0.1 miles to the bikeway parking lot. Pick up the signed Ten Mile Canyon path.

The trail splits almost immediately. Stay right to enter the narrow, craggy Ten Mile Canyon. Follow the path along rushing Ten Mile Creek, watching for bikers who gain high velocity coming downhill from Copper Mountain. Avoid busy weekends here.

Pasque flower, marsh marigold and pussy willow blossom here in late May; red columbine and wild rose in June; lupine and fireweed in July; and raspberries in August.

Two rival narrow-gauge railroads, the gutsy Denver, South Park & Pacific and the aggressive Denver & Rio Grande, competed for ore freight contracts and track right-of-way in the narrow canyon--a battle that erupted in both legal and physical fisticuffs! The bikepath uses the old D.S.P.& P.R.R. roadbed.

Both railroads made numerous mine and town stops along the canyon route. The D.S.P.& P.'s first was the Frisco depot at the base of glory-hole ridden Mt. Royal, near where you entered the bikepath. Next, the Excelsior Mine lies in ruins just 0.4 miles inside the canyon across I-70 on the right. Its massive mill timbers remain clearly visible beside its tailings dump. The railroad also stopped at the King Solomon Mine, its tailings soon seen at trail side on the left. There, energetic early 1900s mine developer, Colonel James H. Myers, drove a tunnel a reputed 11,000 feet into the rock. Just beyond is a gray and brown tailings dump belonging to the big Mary Verna silver mine, with its 1,621-foot tunnel and large power station on the old rail track. Next door stood the Kitty Innes. Beyond the beaver ponds, at 1.9 miles, look for a concrete foundation on the right. This is the site of Curtin, a railroad stop with a one and one-half story log depot. Scattered brick and cabin remnants remain here. Past Curtin, near 2.1 miles, lies the North American Mine. Its steel gray tailings came from a 2,557-foot tunnel.

At about 2.9 miles the railroad stopped at Uneva, where a "Gay 90s" summer resort on the beautiful lake above and northwest became a tourist attraction.

The Admiral and Wonderland Mining Companies operated silver lodes along the next stretch. At Officers Gulch, 3.4 miles, where the highway has an interchange, a lone cabin clings to the canyon's east wall. A wooden tower with an ore tram once stood here, delivering ore to the rail stop from the Monroe Mine high above.

The railroad continued on to the 1880s town of Wheeler (today's Copper Mountain). Located at 6.0 miles, this trail's destination, Wheeler became a frisky sawmill town, with 29 sawmills above in the canyon and a half-dozen within its boundaries. Wheeler also boasted saloons, a billiard hall, blacksmith and wagon shops, notary office, postoffice and a fine hotel with real china dishes--no tin plates. Judge John S. Wheeler, town founder, established the Wheeler Trail (No. 4) to move his sheep to warmer South Park for winter.

Beyond here the path continues over 10,666-foot Vail Pass to the town of Vail.

Take a camera, a fishing pole, a rucksack picnic on this trail and enjoy what Mother Nature, railroad mogul Jay Gould and silver-hungry mining magnates left for your perusal in the steepwalled Ten Mile Canyon. But beware high-speed bikers, especially at view-obstructed spots, and keep children in close check. This trail is not recommended for cross-country ski use due to avalanche danger.

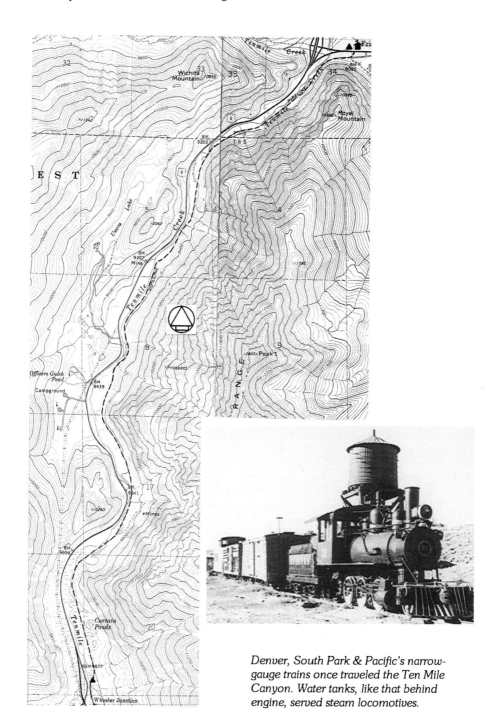

Denver, South Park & Pacific's narrow-gauge trains once traveled the Ten Mile Canyon. Water tanks, like that behind engine, served steam locomotives.

16 NORTH TEN MILE

Time: 5-6 hours
Distance: 5 miles
Elevation gain: 1,700 feet
High point: 10,800 feet
Rating: Moderate
Usually open: June-Sept.
Topo: USGS Frisco 1970, rev. 1987
      USGS Vail Pass 1970, rev. 1987

A fairly easy walk that takes you into the primitive Eagles Nest Wilderness Area, the North Ten Mile Trail penetrates a steep-walled, glacier-carved canyon to its head. Happily for hikers, a combined effort by the Friends of the Eagles Nest Wilderness and the U. S. Forest Service resulted in clean-up of squatter camps here and closure of a road that endured busy 4WD traffic. Now, the North Ten Mile offers serene backcountry enjoyment for hikers and bikers.

Drive I-70 to Frisco exit 201. Turn west into a generous gravel parking area at the overpass west end.

The trail, beginning north of the Frisco town water buildings, climbs sharply at first but levels off to an easy rise. At 0.2 miles notice the ditch leading to a massive early-1900s flume which diverted North Ten Mile Creek water to the impressive placer mining operations of the Buffalo Placers Mining Company in Ryan Gulch, today's Wildernest. (You can see this flume on the side of Chief Mountain from the eastbound 201 on-ramp of I-70.) At 0.75 miles, a waterfall splashes amid mining relics. Look in this area for early-day metal-banded wooden pipe in the creekbed and old timbered water gates in the stream. At 0.9 miles are large beaver ponds. Just beyond, on the right, note tailings from the early 1900s Square Deal Mine. This mine, burrowing into Chief Mountain with three tunnels, earned the title "Crooked Deal Mine" from competitors.

The road undulates through aspen-pine forest to the Wilderness boundary gate at 2.0 miles. A footpath here takes you through dark damp forests latticed with tiny streams into sun-splashed meadows. Look for every kind of subalpine (10,000 feet-plus) wildflower here. We saw wild yellow snapdragons in the September meadow and exquisite red "elegant columbine" in the woods during late June.

Old wagon roads in the area indicate the canyon's mining history. A corral remains near roadside. The canyon's J. D. Hynderliter Ranch belonged to a feisty widower who sat on the Frisco School Board for years--to the dismay of several young schoolmarms who taught in the one-room school house. Old-timers also tell tales of a North Ten Mile Canyon bear who delighted in appearing on the doorsteps of Frisco residents, possibly to get a good scratch against the door frame.

A sign at 3.5 miles marks the Gore Range Trail junction (also called Wheeler-Dillon). Now a rotting corduroy road takes you through three big bogs. This area can get very muddy and hikers have been known to take a tumble into the glup! Avoid the third bog by taking a dry upper path along the hillside. Look for a big tree on the right, with a stump of about four feet to its left. Just beyond this, the trail blurs. Search for the hillside path here.

The trail has no real destination except "trails end", so don't battle the bog if you tire of it. The ridge at the canyon's end marks the county line. The Gore Creek drainage near Vail lies beyond.

Ski touring: *(Moderate)* The initial steep ascent may cause you to question the wisdom of choosing a North Ten Mile tour, but be assured the rest of the trail is a sweet trip through a varied winter landscape. Wichita Mountain, 10,855 feet and Chief, 10,880, stand as sentinels to guard the entrance to the canyon. Farther in, steep slopes present avalanche hazard. But plenty of safe terrain gives skiers a good outing.

On your return, watch the last one mile for fast conditions on the downhill run. A strong snowplow, pole dragging and skiing the trail's snowier edge will help.

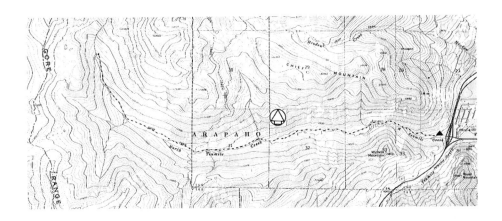

The Square Deal Mine (nicknamed the "Crooked Deal" by critics) dominated early 1900s activity in the craggy North Ten Mile Canyon. The first mile of trail into the canyon served as the mine's ore transportation route.

17 MEADOW CREEK-SALT LICK LOOP

Time: 3 hours
Distance: 5 miles
Elevation gain: 760 feet
High point: 9,920 feet
Rating: Easy
Usually open: late May-Oct.
Topo: USGS Frisco 1970, rev. 1987

A walk in the woods, with lakes, beaver ponds and mining relics along the way, is a refreshing way to spend a free morning or afternoon.

You won't need a car. The route uses the Summit Stage to complete its loop. The trail starts from Frisco's Meadow Creek and ends below Wildernest in Silverthorne. A free bus ride whisks hikers back to the starting point.

Heavy use detracts from the Lily Pad Lakes section of the hike so plan to go mid-week or in the light traffic months of June, September or October. A good early season hike due to its low altitude and sun exposure, this route also makes a splendid autumn hike.

Drive I-70 to Frisco exit 203 and enter the roundabout on the interchange's west side. Exit the roundabout on the gravel road which parallels the I-70 highway. Drive this road to the trailhead. To leave a **second car** at trail's end, drive the Wildernest Road to the Salt Lick Trailhead just south of Wildernest Center. If you don't have a car, ride the Summit Stage to its transfer center near Safeway and cross the interstate bridge to the gravel road described above. Walk 0.6 miles to the trailhead.

The trail climbs at first, a warming ascent through beautiful aspen woods 0.6 miles to the Lily Pad junction. Note the ore chute structure near the Forest Service registration box. Turn right at the junction and travel north on a well-groomed footpath. Now the climb mellows but the trail continues up. Walk alongside rushing Meadow Creek for a short distance to a nice footbridge. A view point on a knobby bluff affords vistas across Lake Dillon to Grays and Torreys Peaks, two Fourteeners on the Continental Divide.

A meadowed slope later provides nice views of Frisco, Bald Mountain and Guyot southeast. Peak One looms behind Mts. Royal and Victoria to the south.

The trail veers right, leaving the creek, and later crosses a rise just before the first of the two lakes. The first lake, alpine in appearance, nestles amid pine and craggy rock. The second, a large pond nearby, puts forth golden Indian pond lilies in July. These lakes lie within the Gore Range Wilderness; please respect the wilderness rules.

Pick up the trail beyond the second lake and follow it 0.5 miles to a junction with the Salt Lick Trail (an acute angle right turn). Look for an irrigation ditch alongside the trail. In this area find the trail that drops down east through a wide cut in the trees to Salt Lick Gulch. Follow the trail through trees to an open meadow with beaver ponds and cabin ruins trailside left. Cross a wooded area and the fence marking the wilderness boundary, then descend another long meadow on closed jeep road that may be muddy in spring. Curve northward and cross Salt Lick Creek, then turn right to follow the road downhill through mixed aspen and pine. Look for wild iris and wild roses in June, columbine and sulphur flower in July. Pass through the gate near the Wildernest Center. New construction has interrupted the trail to Silverthorne, so hikers now walk along the paved road to the fork at Adams. Turn left and continue to 3rd Street to reach the Summit Stage bus stop.

The bus departs twice hourly to Frisco till 6 p.m., then once hourly. Call 668-0999 for details.

Ski touring: *(More difficult)* Ski the snow covered gravel road to the trailhead and use the hikers route all the way to Wildernest Center, where you can catch the free bus.

Bring a map and compass for ski touring in case snow obliterates the trail. At Lily Pad, cross the lake on skis only when ice conditions are reliable. The small lake looks like a meadow in winter; you need to recognize it to find your route. Watch for the junction where skiers meet the Salt Lick Trail 0.5 miles beyond Lily Pad. If ski tracks fail to point the way, look for a wide path heading downhill right. The trail continuing straight ahead goes to upper Wildernest.

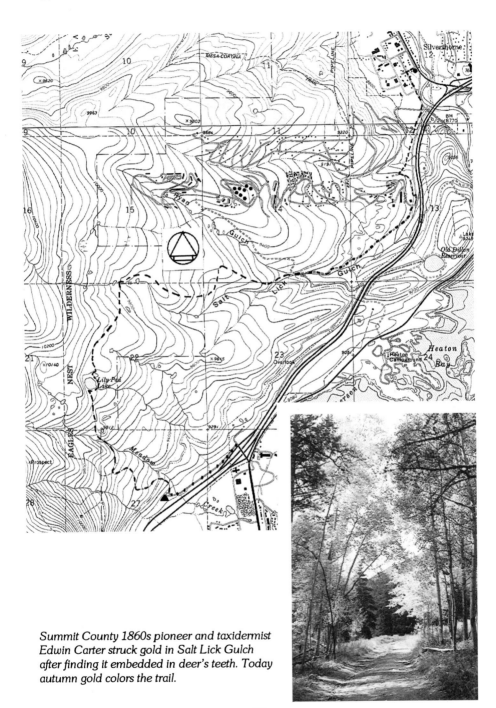

Summit County 1860s pioneer and taxidermist Edwin Carter struck gold in Salt Lick Gulch after finding it embedded in deer's teeth. Today autumn gold colors the trail.

18 MEADOW CREEK-ECCLES PASS

Time: 6 hours
Distance: 4.5 miles
Elevation gain: 2,740 feet
High point: 11,890 feet
Rating: Most difficult
Usually open: July-Sept.
Topo: USGS Frisco 1970, rev. 1987
     USGS Vail Pass 1970, rev. 1987

It's those heady (and hard to get to) high places where the splendor of God's creation is best revealed. While 11,800-foot Eccles Pass above Meadow Creek may challenge your body, its serene beauty will speak to your spirit. Mine relics, rushing Meadow Creek and sweeping views of Lake Dillon east to the Continental Divide peaks will take your mind off the uphill trek enroute.

Drive I-70 to Frisco exit 203. and enter the roundabout on the interchange's west side. Exit the roundabout on the gravel road which parallels the I-70 highway. Follow this gravel road which runs southwest 0.6 to the trailhead.

The trail climbs smartly through pretty aspen groves. Note the curious log building near the Forest Service hiker registration box. The structure has double bins fitted with chutes. Soon a meadow opens up a lovely view of Lake Dillon, often glass-smooth on summer mornings. Pass the Lily Pad Trail junction sign at 0.5 miles. This is the first of three forks, all well marked.

The Meadow Creek Trail continues to climb steadily. After about one and one-half hours of walking, a beautiful valley view unfolds. A mine building lies in ruins at the right and rails for ore cars plus a shaft are on the left. Picnickers will find a great view spot beside rushing Meadow Creek here.

The path levels off in the lodgepole forest. Later, as the timber thins, rock cairns mark the trail. At one point the trail presents a puzzle when a track heading toward Buffalo Mountain seems the right choice. Not so. Follow the cairns.

An expanse of magnificent high meadow at 11,400 feet spreads below Eccles Pass to the north. Look for dainty wildflowers here--buttercup, shooting star, forget-me-not. A sign marks the junction of the Meadow Creek Trail with the Gore Range Trail (called Wheeler-Dillon on the topo map). It comes up between Buffalo and Red Mountain, curves around below Buffalo's steep west face and scales Eccles Pass. This trail continues south to the North Ten Mile Canyon on varied terrain, with streams, ponds, views and an adventurous drop into the canyon.

A steep but exciting climb to the summit of Eccles Pass lets you peer into 12,777-foot Buffalo Mountain's little-seen back yard, a lush beaver-pond dotted bowl. Beyond, look for the Red Buffalo Pass Trail (No. 40) along the staggering rock-strewn slopes of 13,189-foot Red Peak. A note: During some summers the Forest Service posts bear warnings for here.

Frisco miners scrambled over Eccles Pass as soon as winter snows melted, to plumb the silver rich rock walls of Buffalo's north shoulder and Red Peak's south slope. Among them was Frisco's longtime postmaster, Louis A. Wildhack. Meadow Creek and the Red-Buffalo area lay in the Wilkinson mining district, which stretches north to the Grand County line. When miners discovered silver lodes in this area around 1879-80, Eccles Pass began to experience heavy traffic from hob-nailed boots. Today, it lies in silence.

Ski touring/Snow shoeing: *(Most difficult)* Ski the unplowed access road southwest to the Meadow Creek trailhead from I-70 exit 203. Use the hikers' route but watch for avalanche danger if you continue to the above-timberline upper bowls. Call Colorado Avalanche Information 668-0600 or contact the Forest Service in Silverthorne for current avalanche information. The downhill schuss will provide thrills--and maybe some spills.

50

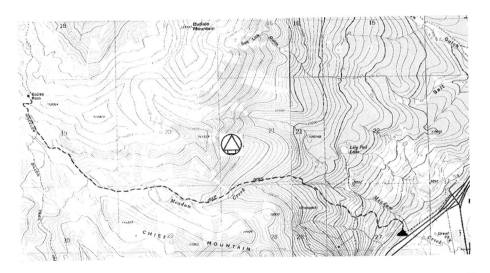

Skiers will glide one-half mile to Meadow Creek trailhead from I-70 exit 203 turnoff. Hikers may drive gravel road to trail parking.

Eccles Pass above Meadow Creek offers view into little-seen bowl behind Buffalo Mountain. The lake-dotted basin attracted silver seekers from 1880s Frisco.

Hikes Around Copper Mountain

19 WHEELER LAKES

Time: 4 hours
Distance: 2.8 miles
Elevation gain: 1,320 feet
High point: 11,080 feet
Rating: More difficult
Usually open: July-Sept.
Topo: USGS Vail Pass 1970, rev. 1987

A stiff climb to a pair of high country lakes unveils views to ancient upper Ten Mile Range peaks, with sculpted canyons, cirques and amphitheatres. In contrast below is busy modern Copper Mountain resort, glistening with green golf fairways and glassy condominiums.

Drive I-70 west toward Vail and take the Copper Mountain-Colorado 91 exit 195. On this exit roadway, approach a bridge, the I-70 overpass. Note the trailhead here, just north of the bridge, before you cross it. Park here if space permits. Or proceed across the bridge, then immediately turn left into the Ten Mile Canyon bikeway parking area. Follow the arrows to the trailhead.

The trail climbs through fluttering aspen glades, alive with wildflowers and mushrooms (late summer). Pretty open meadows offer the first views of Copper's base and the imposing Ten Mile Range south. Enter the Eagles Nest Wilderness at 0.5 miles. Pine forest closes in after about 45 minutes of hiking the steady incline. The trail provides a smooth surface, without the rocks and roots encountered on northern sections of this footpath, the 54.5-mile Gore Range Trail.

Reach a large meadow and enjoy the view west to Vail Pass. Wilder Gulch (hike No. 21) runs southwest near the pass summit. Nomadic Ute Indians used the Vail Pass summit as a hunting ground for almost 7,000 years, according to I-70 excavation discoveries made in the mid-1970s. The Indians traveled Vail Pass enroute to their favorite buffalo hunting haunts in grassy South Park beyond Hoosier Pass.

Ascend to a hilly meadow, enter a pine forest and look for the turn-off to Wheeler Lakes. A Gore Range Trail sign nailed to a tree and a small cairn mark the junction where a 90-degree right turn puts you on a path to the lakes. If the sign happens to be gone when you happen along, look for trees that bend over the trail to make an inverted V arch. A short walk brings you to two mountain lakes.

Mount a knoll above the second lake for an 180-degree panorama from 12,522-foot Uneva Peak and 11,900-foot Uneva Pass across to Frisco and the Dillon Dam road, up past the Dillon Valley residential area to the Eisenhower Tunnel and Continental Divide mountains, then around to the backsides of Peak One and Mt. Royal. (Hike No. 20 crosses Uneva Pass on the Gore Range Trail to Frisco's North Ten Mile Canyon.)

Return on the trail to Copper Mountain, a ski mountain "natural" discovered decades ago but developed and opened in November, 1972. Base land was the old Beeler placer mining claim and, before that, the 1880s town of Wheeler. Judge John S. Wheeler built a sawmill there to supply ties for the Denver & Rio Grande, then constructing railbed down from Fremont Pass. A town sprang up, and though a disastrous fire ravaged Wheeler in April, 1882, the town managed to survive. By 1934, the railroad called the water stop there Solitude, because by then things were very quiet at old Wheeler.

Copper Mountain took its name from a low-grade copper mine near its summit. Beyond

Copper, south to Fremont Pass, lay a stunningly-rich silver mining district, discovered in 1878, that gave two big bustling towns there a lively history. (See *SUMMIT* for the stories of two star cities, Kokomo and Robinson.)

Ski touring: *(Most difficult)* Advanced skiers with a topo map can ski the Wheeler Lakes Trail. The summer path disappears beneath winter's white cover. Returning, the steep downhill drop provides an exciting glissade for experts. Long traverses through the conifers work for the final mile's pitch.

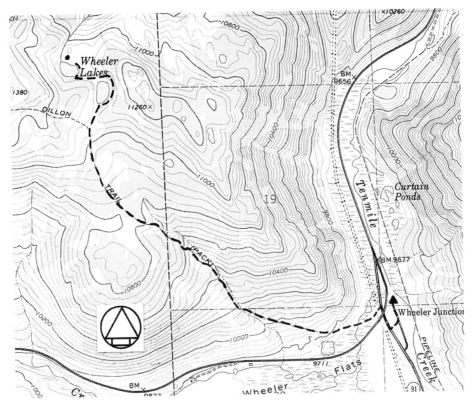

September snow highlights Copper Mountain ski trails and Ten Mile peaks seen from Wheeler Lakes Trail.

I praise thee, for thou art fearful and wonderful. Wonderful are thy works!
Ps. 139:14

20 UNEVA PASS

Time: 7 hours
Distance: 10.75 miles to Frisco
Elevation gain: 2,140 feet
High point: 11,900 feet
Rating: More-most difficult
Usually open: July-Sept.
Topo: USGS Vail Pass 1970, rev. 1987

This little-known and less-used section of the Gore Range Trail remains quiet and beautiful, a 10-mile walk with views of the imposing Ten Mile Range. The path climbs from Copper Mountain to Wheeler Lakes, then past Lost Lake to 11,900-foot Uneva Pass and down to Frisco via the beautiful North Ten Mile Canyon.

Two cars are required for this hike. Leave one car at trail's end, the North Ten Mile Canyon: Drive I-70 to Frisco exit 201 and turn west into the gravel parking area. A road now closed and gated, heads into the North Ten Mile. Park here.

Drive a second car to Copper Mountain using trailhead directions and description for Wheeler Lakes (hike No. 19).

The trail climbs to the turn-off for the lakes at 2.2 miles, marked by a Gore Range Trail sign and rock cairn. Don't turn right here, unless you wish to make the short side trip to Wheeler Lakes. Continue north on the Gore Range Trail, crossing a stream that flows down through Officers Gulch to a lake along the I-70 highway there. An early-day Ten Mile Canyon resident named Officer mined in this gulch. Pass Lost Lake at 3.9 miles and soon begin climbing Uneva Pass, a rise about as steep as the initial section of this trail's ascent from Copper Mountain.

In the Uneva Pass area, watch for a tricky fork in the trail when a distinct path to the right seems an obvious choice, while a faint route dropping down left seems wrong. Go left downhill. Many hikers lose their way at this fork.

The uphill trek to Uneva Pass' summit rewards you with lovely views of the Ten Mile Range and beyond. This silver rich section of the Ten Mile first attracted prospectors in the 1870s. By 1879, Frisco had sprung up. Mines such as the Wonderland, Admiral, North American, Mary Verna, Kitty Innes and King Solomon made the west wall of the Ten Mile Range, visible from Uneva Pass, a rocky anthill full of tunnels and littered with tailings dumps.

By 1881, the Denver & Rio Grande narrow-gauge railway steamed through the canyon below, serving Wheeler, Officers Gulch, Uneva Lake, Curtin, Cunningham and Excelsior between today's Copper Mountain resort (the 1880s town of Wheeler) and Frisco.

The trail drops from the pass summit at 4.7 miles, passing east of Uneva Peak into a marshy area. The trail crosses a stream that drains into the North Ten Mile at the first of these marshes.

Uneva Lake, below and due east of 12,522-foot Uneva Peak here, became a popular dude ranch resort in 1899. Old-timers insisted that no one ever found bottom in the deep glacial lake.

Continue down until you reach the switchbacks that lead into the deep North Ten Mile valley. At the junction of the Gore Trail and North Ten Mile Trail turn right, heading east for 1.5 miles to the Eagles Nest Wilderness boundary gate. Continue another two miles down to Frisco at the mouth of the canyon. You will pass remains of the Square Deal Mine on Chief Mountain at left and pretty beaver ponds at right.

Old-timers remember stories of a cantankerous North Ten Mile cabin dweller who arranged mail-order brides, going through one after another, until Mrs. Lizzie Wildhack changed his ways. When he arrived at the rail depot to meet yet another bride, Lizzie beat him out of Frisco with her broom.

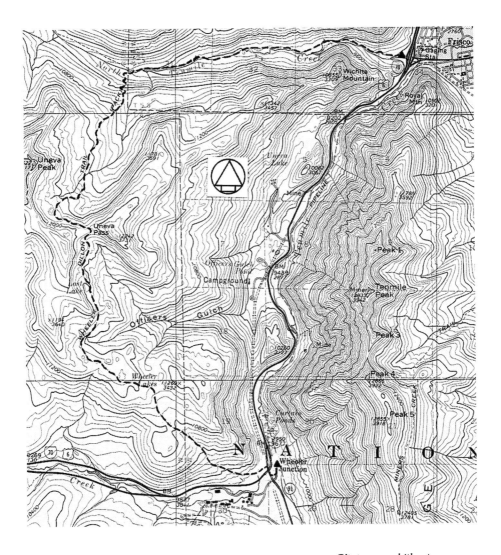

Clinton amphitheater, with Copper Mountain ski runs in foreground, is just one spectacular view on Uneva Pass Trail.

21 WILDER GULCH

Time: 3 hours
Distance: 3.1 miles
Elevation gain: 1,000 feet
High point: 11,500 feet
Rating: Moderate
Usually open: July-Sept.
Topo: USGS Vail Pass 1970, rev. 1987

July 15 to August 1 is peak wildflower time on Vail Pass. Both Shrine Pass above and Wilder Gulch just below offer sun-splashed meadows with many sub-alpine zone flowers. Look for larkspur, snowball saxifrage (kitten's paw), queen's crown, Indian paintbrush and more. Take a picnic to this little-explored valley and enjoy the blossoms on a warm day.

Drive I-70 west past Copper Mountain to the Vail Pass summit. (Look for Wilder Gulch, a valley on the left just below the pass summit.) Turn off at Shrine Pass exit 190. Cross over the interstate and park in the roomy rest stop parking area. Ute Indians used the Vail Pass summit as a hunting campsite for 7,000 years, according to carbon-dated evidence found here during I-70 construction.

The trail begins at the south end of the parking lot and cuts across a brushy slope and grassy rise to drop at 0.5 miles into Wilder Gulch. Reach the footpath, go right and hike uphill on the north-northwest creek bank (right side) along a meadow. The route is an old road but the gulch remains closed to motorized vehicles in summer. When the trail forks, use the upper branch. It affords better views of the spectacular Ten Mile Range and avoids a serious bog on the lower trail. The track stays in the meadow for two-thirds of the hike, then enters conifer forest. Curving through the trees, the path heads up an old telephone line cut, first moderately, then in a steep climb.

In a meadow up high, the trail divides. A right fork follows Wearyman Creek and Turkey Creek to Red Cliff, while a left fork goes over Ptarmigan Pass and drops into Camp Hale. Your path goes left.

Soon you emerge from the trees to view Ptarmigan Hill, a rounded 12,143-foot bump, and Ptarmigan Pass, 11,765 feet. This hike ends on the saddle north of Ptarmigan Hill.

A dirt road winds up to the pass summit. There are two Ptarmigan Passes in Summit County, one here and one near Dillon. This Ptarmigan offers great views of the Saguache Range and the jagged Gore Range-Eagles Nest Wilderness north-northwest. Add-ons to this hike are the short scramble up Ptarmigan Hill (right) or the more advanced climb to the 12,200 foot ridge and higher promontory beyond left.

Ski touring: *(Easy)* Use the hikers' route to access the gulch. Continue right up through the meadows and later the spruce forest, but do not venture into the open snowfields just below Ptarmigan Pass unless the snowpack is stable. On your return, a long, sweet glide returns you to the brief climb over the rise and down to the Vail Pass parking lot.

Resolution Snotours, operated by Vail Associates, runs a snocat in Wilder Gulch on an irregular basis. Peak use is during the Christmas holidays and weekdays, especially in March.

Advanced skiers can use Wilder Gulch to begin a 10.9-mile trip to Red Cliff on a low-avalanche-danger day. Cross the meadow at 2.9 miles, curve right into heavy spruce and fir, then traverse west uphill to cross a flat saddle with a power line at left. Follow Wearyman and Turkey Creeks to Red Cliff. Use maps for this tour.

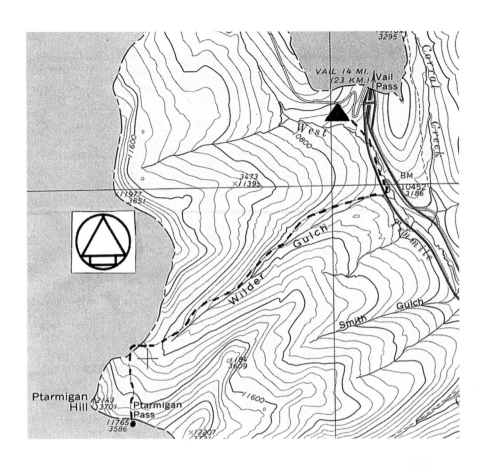

Exploring ruined log cabin provides a breather in Wilder Gulch, nice ski touring terrain.

22 MINERS CREEK TRAIL

Time: 6-8 hours
Distance: 11 miles
Elevation gain: 2,853 feet
High point: 12,573 feet
Rating: Most difficult
Usually open: July-Sept.
Topo: USGS Summit County (North) 1978

A trail along the top of the Ten Mile Range affords unsurpassed views and offers a variety of mountain terrain, from fluttering aspen forest to spartan arctic clime. The hike begins at Copper Mountain and ends at Frisco, where the Miners Creek Trail descends through flower-festooned meadows and woods by sparkling streams. Advanced hikers, acclimated to Summit's altitude, should be in good physical shape for this trek.

Two cars are required for this hike. Leave one car in Frisco at the bikeway parking area, just 0.1 miles east of I-70 exit 201 where the hike will end. (Backpackers may wish to walk the Ten Mile Canyon bikeway back to Copper Mountain, an additional 6 miles.) Then proceed to the trailhead at Copper Mountain.

Drive a second car on I-70 west to Copper Mountain exit 195. Cross the bridge over the interstate and immediately turn left into the Vail Pass-Ten Mile Canyon bikeway parking area. Follow the gas line path 0.25 miles south to the stock drive bridge across from Copper Mountain's steep east-facing A-lift runs. The trail, beginning at left, uses the Wheeler National Recreation Trail to climb to the Miners Creek Trail. Try to hike in dry weather, as this trail stays wet after a rainfall.

The trail rises diagonally southeast across Peak 6's forested western slope, furnishing great views south along the Ten Mile Canyon toward Fremont Pass. The upper canyon yielded millions of dollars worth of silver in the late 1800s. Two bustling towns below Fremont Pass, Kokomo and Robinson, each had 6,000-plus populations. The narrow path rises over 1,500 feet in 2 miles to the Miners Creek junction. Guided horseback trail riders from Copper Mountain's stables may use the first section of the trail.

Cross three streams enroute, the only water until after you cross the Ten Mile crest and drop down toward Frisco. Bring drinking water along. Dry air at high altitude, along with increased respiration, makes strenuous demands on your body's fluid reserves.

At 11,280 feet, 2 miles in, the Wheeler trail links up with the Miners Creek Trail. Veer left here and continue directly east for a stiff climb below the Peak 7 summit. The trail curves at 11,920 feet and heads north behind Peak 7, soon reaching a 12,436-foot elevation. The Wheeler National Recreation Trail crosses the range south (see hike No. 4).

Trekking this top-of-the-world trail along the rocky Ten Mile Range crest leaves you breathless--both from the vast views and the thin atmosphere. The Continental Divide, with Lake Dillon glistening below, the rugged Gore Range, Shrine Pass, Climax, Mount of the Holy Cross and far-off ranges beyond delight hikers as they scale the 12,573-foot Peak 6 summit and continue along at the 12,400-foot level.

Cairns mark the trail, but a topographic map and compass are essential here. A suggestion: Follow the friendly custom of hikers in Nepal. Add a rock to each cairn as you pass. Nepal's alpine cairns reach 10 and 12 feet, nice during unexpected blizzards.

The Miners Creek Trail, constructed in 1936 to connect Frisco to the Gore Trail, descends across Peak 5 to the Ten Mile Range's eastern slope. To the east lies Breckenridge's glittering "Golden Horseshoe", a stunningly-rich gold storehouse that produced the area's famed wire nuggets. (See *SUMMIT* for details.)

A green saddle below Peak 4 overlooks a forest pocketed by pretty meadows. Dip down on a trail well-blazed and groomed for 2 miles to a junction with the Peaks Trail at an early logging camp near 10,000 feet.

Northbound on the Peaks Trail, enjoy rich aspen-pine forest laced with noisy streams and dappled in wildflowers. The Peaks Trail crosses below 12,933-foot Tenmile Peak and 12,805-foot Peak One and parallels the Miners Creek 4WD road. With another 1.5 miles to go, the trail enters the Rainbow Lake district, crossing jeep roads (watch for blue diamond trail markers) and later meets the paved bike route to exit at Frisco's Main Street.

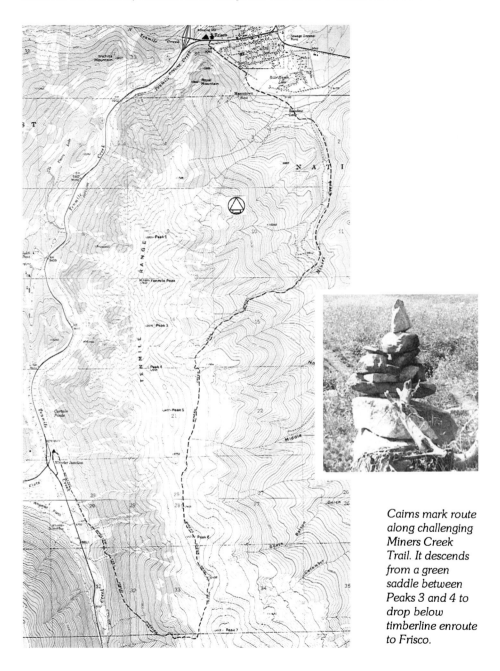

Cairns mark route along challenging Miners Creek Trail. It descends from a green saddle between Peaks 3 and 4 to drop below timberline enroute to Frisco.

23 GULLER CREEK on the Colorado Trail

Time: 6-7 hours
Distance: 6 miles
Elevation gain: 2,200 feet
High point: 12,040 feet
Rating: More difficult
Usually open: July-Sept.
Topo: USGS Copper Mountain 1970, rev. 1987
USGS Vail Pass 1970, rev. 1987

The Colorado Trail in its Guller Creek segment winds alongside a splashing stream in rolling meadows. July wildflowers paint a French-impressionist canvas across the high alpine bowl below Searle Pass, this hike's destination. Half-day hikers can choose a shorter route, ending at the grassy slopes where Guller and Jacque Creeks meet, a nice picnic spot. Unfortunately, development has prompted the Forest Service to re-route the trail across the ski slopes of Copper Mountain. Check the map on page 61 for the trailhead change effective Fall, 2002, when Trailhead A will come into use.

Drive I-70 west past Frisco to exit 195 for Copper Mountain and Colorado 91 south. For Trailhead B, turn right from 91 onto Copper Road and go 1.2 miles through the resort to park at Union Creek. After Fall, 2002, use Trailhead A. Turn left from 91 and park at the Wheeler Flats trailhead lot.

The trail at this writing begins on the Vail Pass bikeway from Union Creek west 0.7 miles to the marked Colorado Trail start. After Fall, 2002 however, hikers will instead walk south .025 miles from Wheeler parking to pick up the Colorado Trail. Then cross Hwy. 91 at the marked crossing and begin the climb up the Copper Mountain slopes. (Add 2.2 miles to the trail's length when using this route. Altitude gain remains about the same.)

The B route enters a riparian valley that's wet and willowy. The A route traverses below Copper lifts with one dip into the resort area for Colorado Trail long-hikers to re-supply.

Both routes reach an early-day camp near Guller Creek where loggers occupied a boardinghouse/mess hall, now in ruins. Loggers harvested trees from the lodgepole pine forest on the valley's right side and the spruce colony on its left. Tall stumps left when sawyers cut trees at snow level were more easily skidded out over the snow.

Hikers who choose the Jacque-Guller Creek confluence as a destination (two log bridges mark the spot) can relax in the rolling meadow here, beneath 13,205-foot Jacque Peak.

Those headed for Searle Pass will enjoy a long meadow which stretches almost to timberline. Switchbacks take you into the trees where the trail climbs to 11,600 feet and emerges into a massive alpine bowl. Cairns guide to Searle Pass at just over 12,000 feet.

As you climb to the pass, you glimpse Janet's Cabin, located less than one mile below Searle Pass. It commands a sweeping view at 11,618 feet. The cabin is available for winter use only, to protect the area's summer elk range, and is reserved for registered guests. Contact the Tenth Mountain Trails Association in Aspen for reservations. Named after Janet Boyd Tyler, an avid skier who died of cancer in 1988, the cabin represents many hours of local volunteer labor.

Views from sandstone-flanked Searle Pass include the Searle Gulch silver mining mecca below. It flourished from 1878 when the notable town of Kokomo sprang up. (See Gilliland's gold rush history, *SUMMIT*, for details.) The impressive Wilfley Mine and Mill, working through the 1950s, the Queen of the West and the Colonel Sellars mines, among others, produced silver fortunes here.

Beyond lie the glacier-carved Mayflower and Clinton amphitheaters and Bartlett Mountain, where the Climax mining operation gouged the peak for molybdenum. This metal strengthens steel and first proved its "mettle" in Word War I. Charles J. Senter discovered the mysterious black-spackled ore in 1879 but struggled 21 years to establish its identity.

Return to your starting point under the guardian flank of 12,000-foot Jacque Ridge, named for Captain John W. Jacque, the ill-starred sidekick of George Robinson, the 1880s mining mogul who dominates area history. When Robinson met his demise, mistakenly shot dead by his own sentry during a mine ownership dispute, Captain Jacque was left to battle for years over his part ownership of Robinson's rich Smuggler mine. No wonder Copper Mountain has named a nearby ski run, "Jacque's Pique."

Ski touring/Snow shoeing: *(More difficult)*. Winter trekkers can choose among several options: Ski the hikers route into the Guller Creek drainage. Or, ride the Union Creek chairlifts and ski alongside alpine runs Roundabout and West Ten Mile to the western ski area boundary gate, then up to the meadow. Skiers who climb as far as Janet's Cabin should respect rental guests' privacy by not approaching the building. Trekkies can climb to Searle Pass at 12,000 feet and enjoy the great ski back down the bowl.

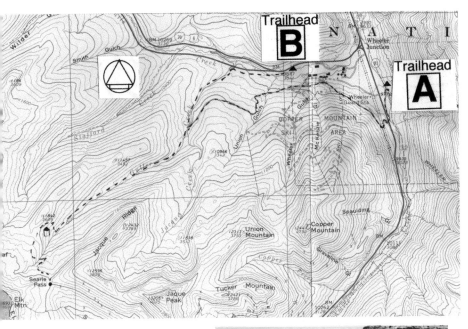

Massive rock marks Searle Pass (foreground) while Gore Range dominates view (background).

61

24 MAYFLOWER TO CLINTON GULCH LOOP

Clinton Gulch Loop
Time: 3 hours
Distance: 5.5 miles
Elevation gain: 1,280 feet
High point: 12,000 feet
Rating: More difficult
Usually open: Late June-Sept.
Topo: Trails Illustrated Breckenridge Tennessee Pass

To Boston Ghost Camp
2 hours
1.8 miles
765 feet
11,645 feet
Easy

Two glacier-carved amphitheaters await hikers on the Mayflower to Clinton Gulch loop. Boston, an early log mine camp, its ruined cabins evocative of another era, makes a nice side trip for the longer hike and a fun destination for an easy, short hike.

Drive Highway 9 south 6.2 miles from I-70 exit 195 at Copper Mountain toward Leadville. Watch for the trailhead on your left. The turn comes up quickly after you glimpse the rock-walled deep valley that is Mayflower Gulch. Turn left carefully and park.

The trail begins on an old ore wagon road and may be shared with jeepers and mountain bikers. On a moderate climb through evergreen forest, you see Mayflower Creek and its adjacent wetlands on the left. Soon signs of Mayflower Gulch's beehive mining history appear: A cabin yard at left displays rusty mine equipment. Later, an ore chute at right shows how miners employed gravity to move heavy ores.

After one mile, the trail begins a gentle descent into the Mayflower amphitheater, a magnificent curve of wild schist-rock ridge with 13,995-foot Mt. Fletcher as its capstone. Northeast, Crystal and Pacific peaks also vie for attention. Notice the fork in the road.

The Boston mine camp once occupied this splendid setting. Now its ruined log boardinghouse and cabins slowly sink into the meadow. Boston hummed with gold mining activity after 1900. The Golden Crest, Golden Eagle and Resumption hard rock mines, as well as the Boston Placers, a surface mining venture, filled the mountain bowl with noise and bustle.

Marv Colsman, who spent his childhood at Boston, returned in 1979 to find his mother's brass bed disintegrating at their cabin site in the abandoned town. A short time later, in the 1980s, gold prices skyrocketed. Miners again worked veins in the stunning basin.

A stop at the ghost camp serves as the destination of an easy 1.8 mile hike. Enjoy, but please help preserve the fragile townsite. Continuing hikers should return to the road fork and begin curving around right to climb Gold Hill, a mineral-rich mount which separates Mayflower and Clinton Gulches. Glory holes, the prospector's trial pits, punctuate the tundra here. The steep scramble to 12,000 feet puts you atop an open, treeless meadow.

Now follow this carefully: Head northwest across the tundra staying on the ridge top and on its north (Mayflower Gulch) side. Views, first of the Gore Range northwest then the Saguache Range west, pop into view. The stunning Clinton Gulch headwall appears. A surreal vista of the Climax Molybdenum Company's tailings settling ponds emerges, an unsettling sight at the site of an 1879-launched silver town, Kokomo, now gone, across the Ten Mile River valley.

Staying north on the ridge top, you will eventually pass through trees, then a meadow and finally arrive at where the ridge top ends and drops into timber. Right here, look for an opening in the trees northwest (left). Enter it; after about 20 feet, it becomes a road. Note a mining glory hole ahead and turn right on this old ore road. It leads down past a mine cabin to Clinton Gulch. Before you reach Clinton Lake, note the dry water ditch off-road at right. This 1.3 mile stretch is the last leg of the loop beginning and ending at the Mayflower Gulch trailhead. Follow the ditch until it swings downhill left. There forge ahead straight and quickly pick up an abandoned mine road. Though young trees grow on the old roadway, pass through them to a drop into the Mayflower trailhead parking lot.

Ski touring/Show shoeing: *(Easy)* The trail protected by conifers, ascends in tunnel-like fashion, then bursts into the snow-laden Mayflower amphitheater. On sunny days, this dazzling bowl, rimmed in gneiss and schist walls, delights. On stormy days, the wind-blasted meadow becomes inhospitable but remains dramatic.

Avoid venturing toward the avalanche-prone headwall. Be sure to check snowslide conditions by calling (970) 668-0600 before you go.

Hiker descending mineral-rich Gold Hill will pass an intact miner's cabin beneath Little Bartlett Mountain. A little farther on, look for the right turn onto the loop-trail's last leg.

25 MT. SNIKTAU

Time: 3 hours
Distance: 1.7 miles
Elevation gain: 1,244 feet
High point: 13,234 feet
Rating: More difficult
Usually open: July-Sept.
Topo: Trails Illustrated Loveland Pass

If you don't own a private plane for perusing Summit's splendid Loveland Pass mountains, the next best thing is to climb Mt. Sniktau.

Views above 13,000 feet are nothing short of spectacular. While the hike's steep first half is a lung buster, there are 100-mile views to savor while you catch your breath. Four ski areas are on display. And the trail's second half is an easier ascent.

Historic Loveland Pass, built as a wagon road in 1879 by William Austin Hamilton Loveland, first served as a commercial route for wagon freight and colorful stagecoaches. Silas Knott ran daily service in Concord coaches drawn by four- and six-horse teams on his popular "High Line" from Georgetown to Summit County and Leadville. Railroad mogul Loveland financed the new route as a lucrative adjunct to his Colorado Central rail company which linked Denver and Georgetown.

Drive Hwy. 6 east to the Loveland Pass summit. Park in the designated area.

The trail begins beside the parking area on the east side of the pass. Since the route lies above timberline, the path is clearly visible mounting the slope ahead. Heavy use on the initial section of the trail has cut a wide swath. Remember that this is alpine tundra, a fragile, heavily-stressed and irreplaceable ecosystem. Please stay on the trail.

The glory of the tundra, especially in July, is its myriad of arctic wildflowers, species that grow nowhere else but a harsh, wind-scoured climate. Look for alpine kittentail, blue sky pilot (it stinks!), blue alpine forget-me-not and yellow old man of the mountain on the grassy lower slopes. Above in the rocky fell fields, note cushion plants that grow in compact mounds to survive blasting winds; their tiny flowers belie their big root size. Moss campion, dwarf clover, both pink flowers, and white alpine sandwort are a few cushion plants.

The trail maintains its steepness to the first summit where huge cairns provide wind shelter. From here 13,427-foot Grizzly Peak rises starkly to the south. Its ridge stretches southeast to famous Torreys and Grays Peaks, soaring skyward at 14,267 and 14,265 feet. East is Kelso Mountain, 13,164 feet.

Views west include 12,477-foot Mt. Trelease; Loveland Ski area; the Williams Fork and Gore Range mountains; the Ten Mile Range; and the Saguache beyond it west; and Arapaho Basin, set against 12,752-foot Lenawee Mountain. Independence and Glacier Mountains tower above the Montezuma area. Notice the Keystone ski area, with its neighbor, Breckenridge, rising beyond across the Blue Valley.

Now the trail turns left for a pleasant and much less taxing ascent of Mt. Sniktau. Be prepared to overtake a second summit (13,152 feet) before the final summit pushes into view. A myriad of alpine flowers, sensational views and a gentler grade make this a rewarding trail segment.

At this writing the trail occasionally faded, leaving hikers to pick their own route. Increased use will remedy this minor problem. Just follow the ridge line. Nearer the summit, rock hides the trail. Again, route finding is easy because the destination is in sight.

Now vistas northward open up. The deeply-carved Clear Creek valley is ribboned by I-70. Above stands Mt. Parnassus (northeast) and Woods Mountain (north). Pettingell Peak juts above Herman Gulch northwest. Traffic whizzing in and out the Eisenhower Memorial Tunnel appears unreal.

Mt. Sniktau served as an alpine ski site for the proposed Winter Olympic Games in the 1970s, a plan defeated by Richard Lamm. Loveland ski lifts operate at the mountain's northwest base.

Due to its steepness, the last part of the return trip is tricky. A good hiking boot with a deep tread makes the descent easier.

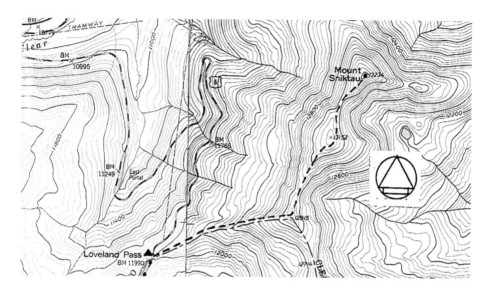

Ptarmigan dwell amid rocks on cloud-catching Loveland Pass peaks.

The heavens declare the glory of God; the skies proclaim the work of his hands. Ps. 19:1

65

26 LOVELAND PASS WEST

Time: 2-3 hours
Distance: 3.2 mile loop
Elevation gain: 489 feet
High point: 12,479 feet
Rating: Moderate
Usually open: July-Sept.
Topo: USGS Loveland Pass 1958, rev. 1987

Summer rests on this lofty basin as briefly as a butterfly on a flower. Snowclogged most of June and bronzed with autumn past mid-August, this ridge-rimmed bowl has only a few short weeks to burst into bloom. Its beauty is worth the wait.

Drive U.S. 6 to the Loveland Pass summit. Park in the marked area.

The trail begins across the road west from the parking area. Notice the high ridge that curves west then north around the alpine bowl. The ridge is your route. With this in mind, go left at the first fork, avoiding the trail that drops right into the bowl.

Two trails ascend the ridge. Stay left and walk along the soaring backbone of the Rockies, the Continental Divide, to a high point at 12,479 feet. Veer right here, following cairns along the ridge. Later, both trail and cairns peter out but the route north is clear. Continue to hike north to a large stone wind shelter at the next high point, 12,276 feet, at 2.1 miles. Hikers end at this view point and return on the same route.

If you're up for a bit of route finding, try the loop down across the green basin, a total hiking distance of 3.2 miles from the trailhead.

To do the loop, drop north a short distance from the high point then make a tight hairpin turn right, hugging the ridge below the summit. Avoid descending the steep slope here. Reach a mini-saddle and look for a bushy draw that is less steep than surrounding terrain. Traverse this down. Keep your eyes on the faraway trail viewed southeast across the bowl. You will meet this trail later. Stay a bit high, crossing streams. Meet the basin trail at the conifer forest.

Hikers planning to do the loop should take a topo map and compass and study the contour lines on the map. The route is not difficult if you choose the proper descent, as indicted by the gentler map contour lines.

Like most areas above timberline, this alpine region can be benevolent--or harsh. Hike early to avoid afternoon electrical storms. Take adequate clothing for wind and weather protection. Don't go if late season snows threaten.

Views from the ridge top above the trailhead include Keystone and Breckenridge ski areas, the towering Ten Mile Range and the Saguache in the distance. The Saguache Range hosts the legendary Mount of the Holy Cross, a cross of snow on a stark 14,005-foot mountain face. Photographer William Henry Jackson sought the cross, immortalized by poet Henry Wadsworth Longfellow. Jackson heard of an 1869 cross sighting from this Loveland Pass area. Finally able to locate the elusive peak, he went on to shoot the Mount's first photograph, using a glass plate negative, on August 23, 1873.

After the trail turns northward, enjoy great views of Loveland ski area, I-70's Eisenhower Memorial Tunnel and the Williams Fork Range, with 12,303-foot Ute Peak as its capstone. (See No. 49 for the Ute Peak trail.) Mt. Trelease and Pettingell lie due north. Below is the Clear Creek valley, striped by I-70. Mt. Sniktau (No. 25) rises east.

Loveland Pass, built in 1879, superseded an earlier pass, 13,132-foot Argentine, this area's first major east-west route. Even after Loveland became the stagecoach and freight leader, rival Argentine stole the winter traffic. The nation's highest Rocky Mountain road crossing, the wind-scoured Argentine was often blown free of snow. But disgruntled travelers sometimes had to crawl on hands and knees to avoid being blown off the pass. As soon as winter's grip loosened, traffic returned to Loveland Pass.

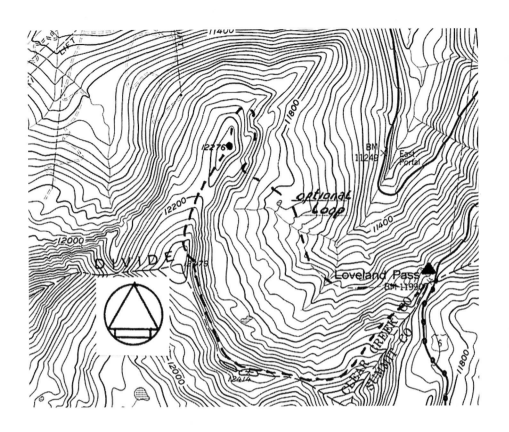

Colorado Mountain College wildflower instructor Nancy Redner explains alpine cushion plants to class exploring Loveland Pass basin.

27 PORCUPINE GULCH

Time: 5-6 hours
Distance: 3.1 miles
Elevation gain: 2,000 feet
High point: 12,000 feet
Rating: Most difficult
Usually open: July-Sept.
Topo: USGS Loveland Pass 1958, rev. 1987

The rugged woodland reaches of Porcupine Gulch protect a natural environment relatively undisturbed by man. The gulch extends from U.S. Highway 6 on lower Loveland Pass up through a well-watered drainage to 12,000 feet, with a range of ecosystems. These include the aspen-pine forest "montane zone" (8,000-10,000 feet); the Englemann spruce-lodgepole pine "Hudsonian zone" (10,000-11,500 feet); and the sedge-moss-lichen-grass "alpine zone" (11,500 feet plus).

Porcupine remains virgin territory because no real trail exists here. Even experienced hikers can expect to get lost a few times. Therefore the hike is rated "Most difficult".

Drive 8.6 miles east from Dillon on U.S. 6 past Keystone. About 3.3 miles past Keystone Lodge on the left (north) Porcupine Gulch opens up. Park below the gulch on the left at a pulloff area with a stone water fountain fed by a cold natural spring. Walk uphill to Porcupine Gulch.

The trail begins on an old logging road following the east side of Porcupine Creek. The route rises steeply at first, but soon softens its sharp rise. The road becomes a trail which climbs through verdant, stream-fed forest land. Rushing along, the creek absorbs little streams that crisscross the trail up higher.

A hide-and-seek trail appears as a beaten track in some places and disappears in lush ground cover in other places. Study the trees for primitive blazes. When you lose the path completely, look for clues. For example, where two weathered logs set across the stream create a makeshift bridge, the trail crosses again to the creek's east side. Plan on spending at least a little time being perplexed in Porcupine Gulch. But don't worry; the mischievous trail always reappears.

Wildflowers abound in mid-summer, especially Indian paintbrush. Every shade, from dazzling pink to crimson, blooms here. Shy arctic gentian, usually a September flower, bloomed here in August.

We reached a large alpine meadow beneath a rocky headwall in 2 1/2 hours of unhurried hiking. Five stream fingers feed Porcupine Creek and hikers can explore each. This hike, however, penetrated the high easterly stream branch shown on the topo map. As you stand surveying the craggy headwall, I-70's Eisenhower Tunnel lies just north beyond the mountains and Loveland Basin ski area lies just northeast.

Porcupine Gulch is named for the same bristly critter that named Porcupine Peak, just southeast across the highway. This peak rises between two branches of the tumbling Snake River, standing as a sentinel to guard the gate to the rich Montezuma silver mining district. Snake River and Peru Creek mines led the nation in silver production around 1900.

Ski touring: *(More difficult)* Porcupine Gulch is not great ski touring terrain. Instead, ski the panoramic route from nearby Keystone Mountain's summit to North Peak. The chairlift ticket is available at a reduced price. End this spectacular tour at North Peak or continue. Other destinations are Ruby lift or the long sweet ski out Keystone Gulch to Soda Ridge Road (16 miles total). For information, maps and lift fees contact the Keystone Cross Country Center.

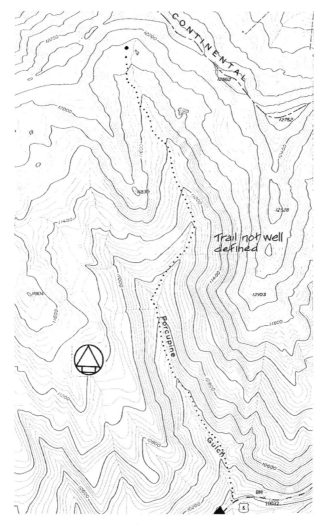

The classic Forest Service blaze, a nationally-used trail marker, does not appear in primitive Porcupine Gulch, where overgrown blazes look like the work of the gulch's namesake.

28 LENAWEE TRAIL

Time: **6 hours**
Distance: **6 miles**
Elevation gain: **2,360 feet**
High point: **12,460 feet**
Rating: **Most difficult**
Usually open: **Mid-July-mid-Sept.**
Topo: **USGS Montezuma 1994**
     USGS Grays Peak 1958, rev. 1987

An eagle's far-flung view from a 12,460-foot high saddle on massive Lenawee Mountain makes a tough trek worthwhile. Half the trail lies above timberline on this challenging tramp from the Peru Creek trailhead up Lenawee Ridge, over Lenawee's crest and down through the north-facing Arapahoe Basin ski area. Bring binoculars.

Two cars are required for this hike. Leave one car at Arapahoe Basin, 12 miles east of Dillon on U.S. 6. Plan to carry water, as the trail provides none. Wear sturdy boots.

Drive 6.5 miles east of Dillon on U.S. 6 to the Montezuma Road (No. 5). Look for Keystone gondola parking directional signs. Turn right. Veer left at the fork, stay right at the next fork and travel on the Montezuma Road 4.6 miles to the Peru Creek Road. The family car can navigate this road, but not until high country snowmelt and mud conditions dry. Proceed on the Peru Road 0.6 miles beyond the bridge crossing Peru Creek to the Lenawee trailhead on the left. Just before the trail sign, you will pass the Maid of Orleans Mine, now a residence, at left. The big Jumbo Mine lies in ruins across the valley. Park off the road beyond the trailhead.

The trail starts at just over 10,300 feet and climbs sharply amid mine ruins for the first 0.75 miles. You reach 10,500 feet at the first left curve. Rock citadels later provide great rest/view spots. You will trek up to 12,250 feet, then enjoy a more gradual ascent.

After reaching the alpine tundra, watch for rock cairns to stay on the trail and also to avoid creating new paths on vulnerable alpine terrain.

At 12,200 feet, just before the gap at the summit, look along the trail for evidence of the American Eagle Mine (also called the Eliza Jane in early days). Located in 1880, the mine produced some rich silver ore from a deep shaft. Just northeast, Isaac Filger's rich Winning Card Mine paid handsome silver profits as late as 1906. Filger dreamed of a resort "city" to be built in the rarified atmosphere near Lenawee's 13,204-foot summit. He built several cabins before abandoning the plan. The Lenawee Trail, earlier named the Argentine-North Fork Trail, served as a pack-mule route to these mines. The *Montezuma Millrun*, an 1880s newspaper, often bemoaned the lack of adequate ore freight transportation in the district, "except the kind in vogue in Old Mexico".

Magnificent views all along this trail open an ever-expanding horizon to include the historic Peru Creek valley, the Sts. John ghost town, Montezuma, Dillon Reservoir and mountains in a sweeping arc beyond. Boulder outcroppings, wildflowers and a possible glimpse of the area's mountain goats add interest to this unique trail.

Steep contours at Thurman Gulch's head pose problems. Walk carefully here to avoid rock slides. The trail drops and rises, resulting in a 200-foot altitude gain.

This hike continues through the gap and then across tundra to connect to a road snaking down through Arapahoe Basin to U.S. 6. (You may choose to return on the 3.3-mile trail back to Peru Creek.) The full Lenawee-to-Arapahoe Basin route totals 6 miles.

Walk the ski area road beneath the chairlift, below Arapahoe's West Wall. At 11,400 feet, the road makes several tight hairpins, then, goes straight to arrive in the valley.

Lenawee, a huge mountain with several summits, dominates the entire walk. Note its famous East Wall on the Arapahoe Basin side, site of a 1983 national speed skiing event. Legend says that big Lenawee took its name from Isaac Filger's tiny daughter, "Wee Lena".

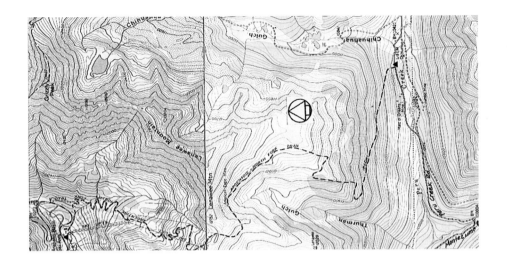

Use binoculars to spy Sts. John ghost town in valley shown. Look for American Eagle Mine remains atop Lenawee ridge. A rock retaining wall, ruins and tailings mark the site. Isaac Filger, 1880 prospector and civic leader, located Lenawee's Winning Card Mine and planned a resort at its summit.

29 CHIHUAHUA GULCH

Time: 4-5 hours
Distance: 3.2 miles
Elevation gain: 1,740 feet
High point: 12,200 feet
Rating: More difficult
Usually open: Mid-July-mid-Sept.
Topo: USGS Montezuma 1994
USGS Grays Peak 1958, rev. 1987

Chihuahua, a town of 200 souls, prospered from its 1879 beginnings till 1889, when the lively community suffered destruction by a raging forest fire. With a U.S. postoffice, two hotels (one named "The Snowslide House"), three restaurants, three saloons and much more, Chihuahua also boasted the best local school in the county. Hard work in nearby silver mines meant hob-nailed boots by day, but at night Chihuahua's frisky townsfolk donned patent leather dancing shoes for elegant parties and fancy-dress balls.

Drive 6.5 miles east from Dillon on U.S. 6 past Keystone Lodge to the Montezuma Road (No. 5). Look for the Gondola Parking sign. Turn right, then veer left at the fork and proceed 4.6 miles to the Peru Creek Road. Take a sharp angle left. The family car will navigate this road after spring runoff. Follow the road about 2 miles to the Chihuahua Gulch 4WD road junction at left. Pass the Maid of Orleans Mine, now a home at left, the Lenawee trailhead and the Jumbo Mine and Mill across the valley. Park beside the road.

The Chihuahua Gulch hike begins at the now-silent site of old Chihuahua and climbs 3 miles to a pristine glacial lake. The hike uses a 4WD road, closed above the Ruby Gulch turnoff.

Investigate the century-old cemetery on a hillside east of Chihuahua Gulch. A number of simple graves sleep amid charred timber, evidence of the town's fiery 1889 demise. The Chihuahua schoolhouse was located next to the graveyard and children scampered among the mounds, according to old-timers.

The trail rises relentlessly at first, then becomes gradual. A road intersects, but the trail stays left. Crossing the creek can prove tricky, depending on the flow when you hike. Pass two strings of beaver ponds connected by the stream in a marshy area. Dry socks and even extra shoes are sometimes a blessing on this trail! Try August for lower stream flow.

Keep left at the next fork, a road at 11,200 feet which leads to private property in Ruby Gulch. Watch for the tricky fork that occurs at a creek crossing.

Emerge into the open meadows above timberline for the last section of trail curving left enroute to 12,200-foot Chihuahua Lake. The track has crossed a stream, which flows from the lake. Although you cannot see the lake, it is directly west above the trail. A steep scramble up a grass and talus slope leads to the tarn, which may still be frozen on July 4!

Chihuahua Gulch, dominated by surrounding mountains, has huge Lenawee as its west wall, 13,427-foot Grizzly Peak at its head and two Fourteeners, 14,270-foot and 14,267-foot Grays and Torreys Peaks, to the east. A herd of mountain goats pastures on Grays Peak and meanders across Chihuahua Gulch to Lenawee in summer.

Ski touring: *(More difficult)* We rated this gentle trail "More difficult" because Peru Creek ranks as one of Summit County's prime avalanche areas. Severe danger exists near trail's end (5 miles) where the 1800s town of Decatur was smashed by a slide off Grays Peak in 1898. Less severe, but significant, danger exists below Chihuahua. It takes mountaineering knowledge and a current avalanche report to make a safe tour here.

The gentle Peru Creek Road winds through snowy aspen woods into the historic silver-rich Peru valley on a popular cross-country ski route. Begin at the Peru Creek turnoff, 4.6 miles in on the plowed Montezuma Road. Park here and follow the unplowed roadbed through the trees. The valley soon opens up. You pass mine relics and cross the Snake

River, then overtake the Lenawee hiking trail (No. 28) at left. The Chihuahua site, with a 4WD road climbing the gulch at left, marks the 2.0-mile point. The ski trail continues all the way to the Horseshoe Basin, a 5-mile-plus tour, where avalanche danger is extreme.

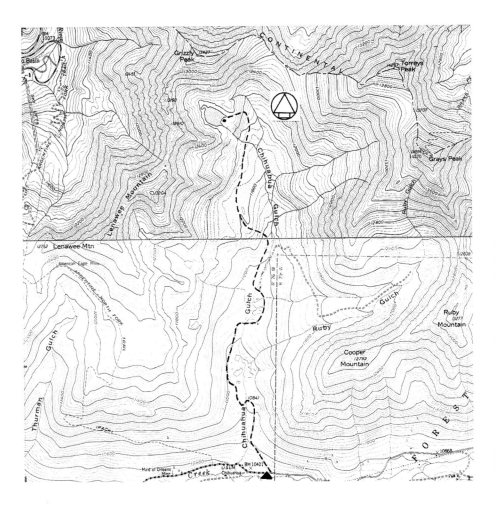

Crossing Chihuahua Creek presents a challenge during runoff or rainstorm. Go left at watery fork shown below.

30 ARGENTINE PASS

Time: 3 1/2-4 hours
Distance: 2.3 miles
Elevation gain: 2,110 feet
High point: 13,207 feet
Rating: Most difficult
Usually open: Mid-July-mid-Sept.
Topo: USGS Montezuma 1994
     USGS Grays Peak 1958, rev. 1987

Both the dreams and despair of the 1860s prospectors are expressed in the colorful history of Argentine Pass. Contrasted with the determined dream of providing Peru Creek silver miners a freight access to Denver were the grim realities of a near-impossible task in building America's highest Rocky Mountain road crossing. Tragic loss of life and property shadowed its construction and use. Road crews simply walked off the job when faced with the pass' perpendicular west slope. But never-say-die promoter, Stephen Decatur, pushed Argentine Pass over the Continental Divide to completion in 1869.

The hike to Argentine's soaring 13,207-foot summit taxes the body but restores the soul. To accomplish the 2-mile trek from 11,097 feet in the raw, rocky Horseshoe Basin to Argentine's dizzying crest becomes a personal achievement. Views, below to the mine-riddled Peru Creek valley, across to towering Grays and Torreys Peaks and west to the Mount of the Holy Cross and ranges beyond, make the spirit soar.

Bring plenty of water, wear sturdy shoes or boots for shard rock and bring warm clothing. Hikers can begin this trail in shorts and shirt sleeves and end wearing ski hats, jackets, vests, pants and mittens. Begin the hike early, planning to return before 1:00 p.m. when electrical storms often occur. Lightning above timberline may cause dangerous ground currents.

Drive U.S. 6 east from Dillon 6.5 miles to Montezuma (Gondola) Road (No. 5). Turn right, veer left at the fork and go 4.6 miles to the Peru Creek Road. Make a sharp left and follow this road about 5 miles to a trailhead parking area at the Shoe Basin Mine building on the right. Walk 0.3 miles up to the trailhead, marked: "Argentine Trail-Summit, 2 miles".

The trail, a one-time wagon and stagecoach road, crosses the creek and swings right. You can pick out the path of the 1860s route rising along the shard-rock wall of 13,738-foot Argentine Peak. Mount a steep incline at first, then pace yourself to a more gradual but unrelenting upward climb.

Look for a miniature garden of alpine wildflowers in tiny nosegays on the lower part of the trail. Above lies a windswept world with little vegetation except for the perverse thistle.

The trail loops once, giving hikers a long look at a pretty meadow between Argentine Peak and neighboring Decatur Mountain, 12,890 feet. Then the path heads northeast all the way to the summit, crossing talus. Notice the Horseshoe Basin mines, including the National Treasury on the east side of the road below and the Peruvian and Paymaster on the west side. Above the Paymaster lies the Falls Gulch lake. The Vidler Tunnel's buildings appear below. Around the turn of the century, Britisher Rees Vidler took a notion to tunnel below the Continental Divide. The goal: A railroad route from Georgetown to Peru Creek and Montezuma. After a herculean effort, tunnel excavation stopped just short of completion and never resumed. Today, the Vidler Tunnel is used for water diversion.

Argentine Peak, on your right as you climb, begins an arc that includes 13,850-foot Mount Edwards, then 14,270-foot Grays, 14,267-foot Torreys, 13,427-foot Grizzly and 13,277-foot Ruby Mountain. The two Fourteeners were named for famous botanists, Asa Gray and John Torrey.

Nearing the summit, the trail enters a gray granite world of rock. Scan it for remains of the 1880s Silver Queen Mine. Airplanes enroute to the West Coast slice overhead amazingly close! Stark, jagged surroundings heighten a surprise on crossing the summit on the Continental Divide. There you suddenly see green tundra, rounded, rolling mountain tops and a wooded valley down toward Georgetown.

Just beyond the summit on Argentine Pass' east side are good spots for a rucksack lunch. Watch for grasshoppers on the snow. A never-ceasing wind scuds across the top, a reminder that early-day winter travelers often had to crawl over the wind-scoured Argentine summit on hands and knees--to avoid being blown off!

Inset: Colorful local character Stephen Decatur built "impossible" Argentine Pass and an 1860 silver town its 11,000-foot base.

Skyscraping Argentine Pass, an 1860 stagecoach and wagon route, rises to 13,207 feet. Top of signpost points to pass summit.

31 SAPPHIRE POINT

Time: 15 minutes
Distance: 0.8 miles
Elevation gain: nil
High point: 9,500 feet
Rating: Easy
Usually open: June-Sept.
Topo: USGS Frisco 1970, rev. 1987

An easy, fun trail, Sapphire Point Loop is short, perfect for families with young children or visiting Grandmas. The trail is not short on views however. Dramatic views of Dillon Reservoir, a sheer drop below, and commanding Buffalo Mountain beyond make this level path one to remember.

Drive to Swan Mountain Road (No. 1) either south 3 miles from Frisco on Colorado 9 or east 3.4 miles from Dillon on U.S. 6. Take Swan Mountain Road to its highest point, where a parking area is anchored by a huge boulder bearing a plaque to commemorate road completion in 1966. Park here and begin the loop from trailheads at either corner of the parking area.

The trail, using the south entrance, leads first to a stone-walled lookout area perched on a cliff high above the lake. From this vantage point, survey the reservoir. Below lies a place that early explorers remembered--a place where three rivers met and became one. Trappers' rendezvous were held here, at "La Bonte's Hole". To the south, Dillon's Blue River arm extends to Farmers Korners, near the site of old Dickey, a railway coaling station on the narrow-gauge that traveled from Breckenridge to old Dillon. Frisco Bay also stretches south to Frisco, founded in 1879. Below 12,777-foot Buffalo Mountain, the site of old Dillon now rests beneath the water. Dillon, an 1870s log settlement, became a crossroads for early toll roads, stagecoaches and, in the 1880s, two narrow-gauge mountain railways. Old Dillon once spread in the flat valley just below the glory hole south of the dam. The town became a commercial center, supplying ranches on the lower Blue River with retail goods.

Dillon had a newspaper, the *Blue Valley Times*, hotels, saloons, U.S. postoffice, general store, school and challenging local ski jump.

Moved to make way for the Denver Water Board's diversion project, Dillon relocated on a hill above the reservoir in the early 1960s. The dam was topped on July 18, 1963. Surprised engineers watched water from the Snake, Blue and Ten Mile rivers, which feed the lake, rise at a rate of six feet per day. In August, 1965, the 25-mile perimeter lake stood full. Water, diverted through the Roberts Tunnel beneath the Continental Divide, flows to Denver via the South Platte River.

The Sapphire Loop curves around 9,606-foot Sapphire Point hill, along an open stretch and then into the trees before trail's end.

Ski touring: *(Easy)* Scenic Windy Point, located just below and east of Sapphire Point, lies in the Swan Mountain Recreation area. The area, like its neighbor, Sapphire Point, enjoys great Lake Dillon views. Drive 0.8 miles below Sapphire Point on the Dillon-Summit Cove side of Swan Mountain Road. The trail along the snow-covered closed roadway passes the turnoff to the Prospector campground and heads straight northwest one mile to Lake Dillon's Windy Point. Initial views are to Frisco's silver-rich Chief and Wichita Mountains and to round-topped Buffalo, then across the frozen lake to 12,498-foot Ptarmigan Mountain.

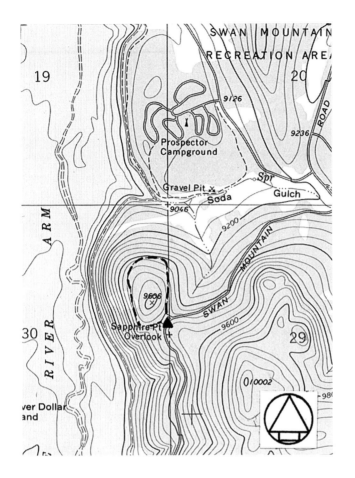

*Domed Buffalo
Mountain dominates
semi-circular
panorama across Lake
Dillon from Sapphire
Point. Recent trail work
rendered the path
wheelchair-accessible.*

32 TENDERFOOT MOUNTAIN

Time: 1-2 hours
Distance: 1.25 miles
Elevation gain: 520 feet
High point: 9,800 feet
Rating: Easy-moderate
Usually open: June-Sept.
Topo: USGS Dillon 1970, rev. 1987

Can't wait to start the hiking season? When snow still clogs the high trails, try Tenderfoot. This short south-slope trail melts off early, provides expansive views and offers a variety of vegetation for a "nature trail" experience.

Drive east from I-70 Silverthorne exit 205 to the Dillon stoplight on U.S. 6. Turn left toward the Lutheran Church, then take an immediate right on the eastbound roadway parallel to U.S. 6. Travel 0.5 miles on this road past the U.S. Forest Service compound and shop. Proceed onto the dirt road toward the Dillon water tank and designated trail parking on a side hill below the tank. Do not block water facility access. A dirt road above the water tank over the hill leads past the administration building 0.25 miles to the trailhead.

The trail begins near a wire fence with a gate to the uphill footpath. A sunbaked rocky hillside provides a perfect habitat for pungent blue-gray sagebrush and olive-green bitterbrush. The two are often found together. Bitterbrush becomes the most important browse plant for deer in winter. This plant produces pale yellow flowers in late June.

An aspen colony, with abundant wildflowers on its damp forest floor, is the next ecosystem on the nature trail. Aspen saplings spring from connector roots. Aspen groves, connected below the surface by interlaced roots, usually climb uphill from a stream or lake. Look for blue columbine, purple lupine, and purple mountain larkspur.

Soon the "peckerpoles", a lodgepole pine community, crowd in against the trail. A rusty, pine needle-carpeted forest floor here receives little light to nurture groundcover. Ute Indians prized the narrow, straight pine trunks (those a bit thicker than the skinny peckerpoles) for tepee construction. Hence, the name, lodgepole.

The trail completes a big hairpin curve, heading southeast, then north, then southeast again. Above the pine forest, the sunny hillside trail opens up views of the Gore and Ten Mile Ranges, plus a panorama of Lake Dillon with the marina below. Benches enroute offer rest stops.

The third bench provides vistas west to the soaring Gore Range, across the reservoir southwest to 12,805-foot Peak One, then down the Ten Mile Range to the Breckenridge ski area and southeast beyond Summit Cove toward the Continental Divide.

Strollers, camera bugs and families may take longer, but a paced walk to trail's end requires only 30 minutes. Sweeping views at the top make you want to linger there.

Tenderfoot Mountain, 11,441 feet, dominates the Dillon area and is one of the few big Summit County mountains that has its summit below timberline. Tenderfoot never experienced much prospector activity. The only significant mining near Dillon took place at the big Oro Grande pit, where an Evans hydraulic elevator assisted placer mining deep below the surface.

Ski touring: *(Easy)* Knockout views reward skiers on the Tenderfoot Road. The tour follows the road and passes the hiking trail gate (the trail is not skiable) to continue 2.5 miles along the snowy roadway. Continue past the Dillon Cemetery to a wooden closure north of the Summit Cove residential area across Hwy. 6. Several forks occur: When faced with two visible roads heading east (avoid the road climbing north into a valley), choose the higher road. Choices occur at the power lines and again where skiers face a gentle uphill left or a gentle drop right. Go left both times.

This sun-blessed trail melts quickly. Go December-February after a snow on cold days.

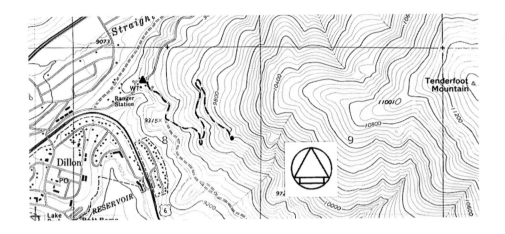

Forested Tenderfoot Mountain stretches long (but low 11,441 feet) over Dillon Dam and Reservoir.

Below: Peak 1 rises as a sentinel above Dillon Reservoir, one of many views from Tenderfoot Mountain.

33 OLD DILLON RESERVOIR

Time: 1 hour
Distance: 0.2 miles
Elevation gain: 160 feet
High point: 9,200 feet
Rating: Easy
Usually open: May-Oct.
Topo: USGS Frisco 1970, rev. 1987

A great hike for kids...a nostalgic walk for those who remember Old Dillon...an easy first-hike-of-the-season...a lunch hour getaway for local office workers...and a dramatic Buffalo Mountain view spot. All these advantages make this easy trail attractive. Take a picnic and mellow out at the "lake above the Lake".

Drive the Dam road 1.5 miles from the Frisco entry or 2 miles from the Dillon entry. The trailhead is marked and has its own parking.

The trail climbs northwest to the lake at 9,200 feet. From the trail hikers view Lake Dillon with Swan Mountain (east) and Tenderfoot (northeast) standing as sentinels. Beyond east is the Continental Divide. At the lake an old road curves around the lake's north shore, a good route for young explorers.

Many varieties of wildflower bloom in the lake's meadow location. Buffalo Mountain, 12,777 feet, looms close. Hikers get a good view of the cleft between Buffalo and 13,189-foot Red Peak. The deep valley serves as the route to South Willow Falls (No. 39) and the challenging Red-Buffalo Pass trip to Vail (No. 40).

Old Dillon's site lies submerged beneath the waters of Dillon Reservoir, completed in 1963. The town served as a crossroads, first linked to the outside by 1870s wagon roads and stagecoaches, then in the 1880s by two rival narrow gauge railways, the Denver & Rio Grande and the Denver, South Park, later called the Colorado & Southern. Though Dillon occupied a unique site where three rivers met, early day townsfolk built ditches from the Buffalo-Red Peak area creeks to create their town reservoir.

Old Dillon spread out below today's Glory Hole on Dillon Dam. Residents moved to the town's present location on the Lake's north shore during dam construction starting around 1959.

The old reservoir sits in a meadow on Old Dillon's Lake Hill where 1920s ski jumper Anders Haugen set a world record soaring 214 feet from the Dillon Jump. The road meanders around to climb Lake Hill where a precipice above Lake Dillon and the Glory Hole provides sheer-drop views. This is the ski jump site. A U.S. government communications facility atop Lake Hill warns visitors of danger due to high voltage.

Ski touring: *(More difficult)* Skiers will enjoy nice views of Silverthorne and Buffalo Mountain along with the Lake Dillon vistas on a mid-winter tour. (The snow is too thin both early and late season to provide good touring, especially on the difficult steep road sections.)

At this writing, the best Lake Hill ski route begins at the Dillon Dam's southwest edge, on the closed road just across the road. Snowmobiles use this road for regular service to the communications facility but their use is limited. The climb is steep but rewarding. Skiers can also use the hiking trail route but it is somewhat difficult to find when snow covered.

The U.S. Forest Service plans to make the Lake Hill hiking trail handicapped accessible. At that time, the trail will be a wide path, easily discernable in winter. Then the trail will become the choice route for ski touring. The rating will then change to "Easy."

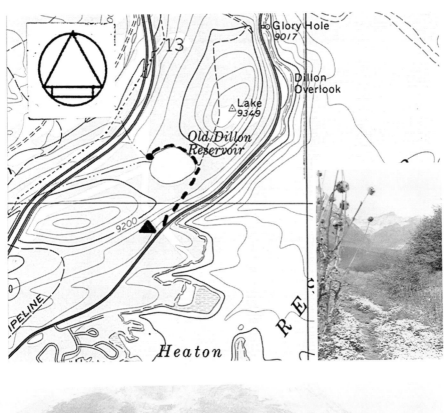

Buffalo Mountain looms over Old Dillon Reservoir. Inset: Wildflowers border trail.

34 PTARMIGAN MOUNTAIN

Time: 6 hours
Distance: 4.6 miles
Elevation gain: 3,098 feet
High point: 12,498 feet
Rating: More difficult
Usually open: Late June-mid-Sept.
Topo: USGS Dillon 1970, rev. 1987

Climbing Ptarmigan Mountain makes an exhilarating outing with all the forest beauty and knockout views hikers love. What's more, the trail is padded like a carpet store showroom, soft with built-up mulch, and rock-free.

The hike enters the new Ptarmigan Peak Wilderness Area, a federal wilderness established in 1993. For that reason, mountain biking is prohibited at the wilderness boundary near the summit and wilderness regulations apply.

The Forest Service and local homeowners have teamed up to solve a longtime access problem. Hikers can now relax and enjoy the trail's abundant wildflowers instead of searching for the route.

Drive Colorado 9 to Silverthorne's Tanglewood Drive (next to Wendy's), just northwest of I-70 exit 205. Proceed 0.2 miles, past the hotels to road No. 2021. Turn right and drive 0.9 miles to a pull-off before the left-hand curve in the road. Park.

The trail begins in aspen trees and crosses a road to regain the footpath.

The track leads through a dry, rocky, sagebrush area and connects briefly with an overgrown road which takes you through a gate. Both the 4WD road and a footpath climb to Ptarmigan's 12,498-foot summit. Cross the road, which climbs sharply, and use the trail, rising gently to enter a rich aspen forest.

As you gain altitude, take a breather to look back on Lake Dillon, shimmering like a jewel in its mountain setting. To the west, Buffalo Mountain and Red Peak loom large, giving you a great view into Red Buffalo Pass, site of this book's hike No. 40. Soon, you can see all the way south to the Breckenridge ski trails on the Ten Mile Range. The trail continues up and north in pine forest, which opens to reveal the gentle lower Blue River valley and the imposing Gore Range.

Three streams cross the trail. Look along dark forest stream banks for ptarmigan who come to drink.

Ptarmigan hikers gain a walloping 3,098 feet in altitude, more than any other hike in this book except Quandary Peak, a Fourteener. But the increase is spread over 4.6 miles so the hiker does not experience it as a punishing climb. At about 11,500 feet hikers enter the Ptarmigan Peak Wilderness.

Watch for a trail descending from Ptarmigan Pass, northeast at 11,777 feet, which meets the Ptarmigan Trail at about 11,500 feet. This trail provides the link in an 8.4-mile loop trip that connects Ptarmigan and Laskey Gulch trails. (See hike No. 35 for details on Laskey.)

The path ascends to above timberline and then, quickly to the 12,498-foot Ptarmigan Mountain summit. Once on the open rolling tundra, the trail joins the jeep track.

Atop Ptarmigan, towering Grays and Torreys Peaks on the Continental Divide dominate the view east. Northwest of Torreys, the Loveland Pass area appears. Beyond Tenderfoot Mountain spreads residential Summit Cove, site of the late 1800s Rice Ranch. Just below lies the green cut of Laskey Gulch, stretching to its head at Ptarmigan Pass.

North of the summit, a ridge along the Williams Fork Range rises. The Ptarmigan Trail also completes a difficult but rewarding hike from Ute Pass, 12 miles north of Silverthorne, up Ute Peak and along this ridge and down Ptarmigan to the Lake Dillon area. (See hike No. 49.)

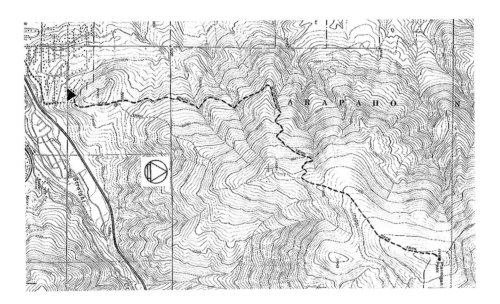

Kids take a break by stream on Ptarmigan Mountain.

Below: Enroute to Ptarmigan's summit, trail enters Ptarmigan Peak Wilderness. At top hikers can connect to Ute Peak Trail traveling north along Williams Fork Range crest to Ute Pass area.

35 LASKEY GULCH

Time: 5-6 hours
Distance: 2.8 miles
Elevation gain: 2,327 feet
High point: 11,777 feet
Rating: Most difficult
Usually open: July-Sept.
Topo: Trails Illustrated Vail-Frisco-Dillon

Seven stream branches, like seven laughing sisters, course down through lush, forested Laskey Gulch. Idyllic beauty in virgin woodland, dappled with delicate wildflowers, will entice the hiker. But a perverse path that drowns in bog, vanishes at meadow crossings and hides amid a maze of game trails may cause that same hiker to curse this lovely, frustrating spot.

Drive I-70 east 5.5 miles from Silverthorne exit 205 to "The Box", a highway turn-around. Pass beneath I-70 and proceed west to the lower of two truck runaway ramps. Just around the curve below this ramp, 2.6 miles from "The Box", is a small pull-off area for Laskey Gulch. Slow down with care and park well off I-70.

We consulted the Colorado State Patrol about parking. The Highway Department has bulldozed a berm to discourage cars. The Patrol will not ticket here but will issue a 24-hour warning tag if congestion occurs. Idea: Ask a friend to drop you off.

The trail climbs from 9,450 feet at the highway to 11,777-foot Ptarmigan Pass, on the Summit-Grand County line. Traversing dry streambed, marsh, forest, meadow and hill, the elusive path crosses the main stream and smaller ones several times. The USGS Dillon map shows no trail in Laskey Gulch, but *Trails Illustrated,* sold locally, has the route and its connection to the Ptarmigan trails. This map identifies the path along the easterly stream branch--if you keep this noisy stream within earshot, you should not get lost.

Flowers abound in the green gulch, where ground cover spreads over every inch of forest floor. Wild rose, lupine, monkshood, chimingbells and Indian paintbrush (this in vivid hues of lavender, purple, rose and red) grow everywhere. Mushrooms in August vary from button to saucer size, some fluted and curled, in shades of copper, gold and orange. In wet areas, many varieties of moss, in bright lime and rich emerald, flourish.

Laskey Gulch draws its name from the John Laskey family, Cataract Creek ranchers who built a sawmill high in this gulch. Today it is part of the new Ptarmigan Peak Wilderness.

Reach the high meadows and look back to see magnificent views of Dillon Reservoir, Peak One and the Ten Mile Range, Breckenridge ski area and the gold-rich mountains east of historic Breckenridge. Upper meadows display ruby-hued little red elephant flower, each petal resembling an elephant's head and trunk, kitten's paw and columbine.

The gulch narrows at treeline and you can see the tundra-covered ridge where Ptarmigan Pass crosses. Now true alpine flowers vie for attention, including ruby king's crown, white candy tuft, blue alpine forget-me-not and pink dwarf clover. Especially here, the tundra is like a big sponge. The source of the stream lies in a spring near the ridge top.

Ptarmigan Pass earned legendary status when greenhorn prospector Tom Dillon, half-crazed from the hardship of wintering lost and alone in the high country, crossed the summit to drop into a valley where three rivers met. The valley later sprouted a town named Dillon, known for the confluence of the Snake, Ten Mile and Blue Rivers.

A trail cutting northeast across the rise reaches the pass, where a sign indicates trails to Straight Creek and the Williams Fork mountains. "Straight Creek-7 Miles" refers to a route southwest along the ridge connecting to the Ptarmigan Mountain Trail (5.8 miles down Ptarmigan and another 1.1 miles through a residential area to Straight Creek).

For a delightful 8.4 mile loop trip, climb Laskey Gulch, cross the ridge and descend Ptarmigan Mountain. (See hike No. 34 for Ptarmigan directions.)

THE NEW
SUMMIT HIKER
AND SKI TOURING GUIDE
TRAIL MAP

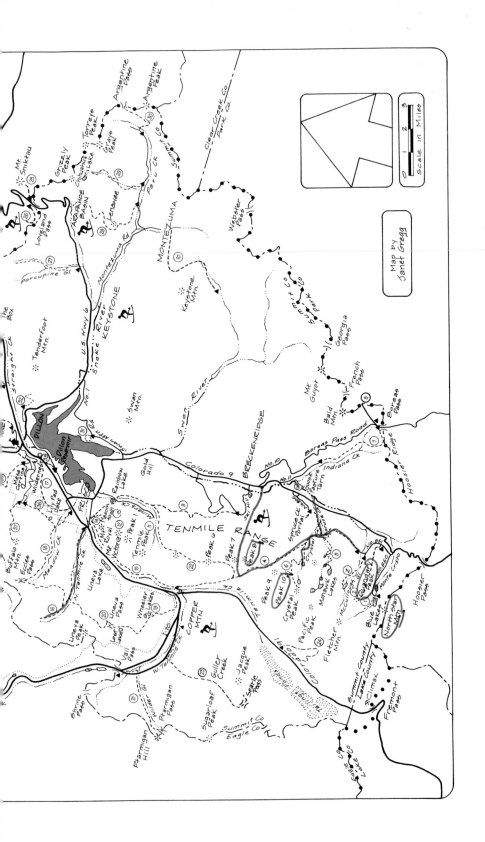

Map by
Janet Gregg

Scale in Miles
0 1 2 3

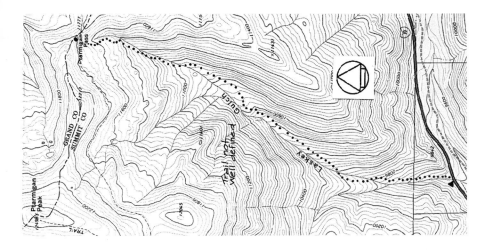

Laskey Gulch Trail leads to Ptarmigan Pass, a route to the Williams Fork drainage.

36 LILY PAD LAKES

Time: 1 1/2 hours
Distance: 1.6 miles
Elevation gain: 200 feet
High point: 9,920 feet
Rating: Easy
Usually open: June-Sept.
Topo: Trails Illustrated Vail-Frisco-Dillon

Lower Lily Pad Lake wears a mantle of sunshine-yellow Indian pond lilies in late July. Upper Lily Pad, fed by a noisy stream, resembles a picture postcard alpine lake. Together, they make a good destination for a family hike and a nice cruise for cross-country skiers.

Drive beyond the Silverthorne I-70 exit 205 north on Colorado 9 to the Wildernest Road, opposite Wendy's. Turn left at the 7-11 store and continue 3.5 miles up through the subdivision and around the final upper loop. Near the top, note a sign for the South Willow Trail. Pass that and just beyond the top of the loop, see a road leading up to Wildernest water tank No. 6. Park and walk up the hill to the trailhead right of the buried water tank.

The trail travels south, crossing small streams and skirting beaver ponds, through heavy aspen and pine forest to the two lakes.

Curve left around the first beaver pond, then cross the unpeeled log walkway through a bog. Bring insect repellent for this sometimes buggy section. Pick your way through the boulder fields, curious remains of Ice Age glaciers and freeze-thaw action.

A chain of beaver ponds near Lily Pad and below attracted fur trappers during the fur trade boom years, 1810-1840. Dillon Reservoir water covers the site of historic La Bonte's Hole, a Rocky Mountain trappers' rendezvous spot. Summit County's natural beaver habitat made the area a prime trapper target. Its high altitude assured a thick, heavy coat on the beaver. Better pelts made for better profits and more luxurious beaver fur hats, the gentlemen's fashion accessory of the early 1800s.

The trail follows an irrigation ditch on clay subsoil built up here by the water-hungry Buffalo Placers Mining Company, an early 1900s venture that used hydraulic placer mining techniques in Salt Lick Gulch just below.

After a big dip on the trail, you climb to the first, smaller lake. Notice the many birds along this well-watered trail, especially at the lake. The larger second lake makes a fun place for families to explore.

Extend the hike, if you wish, by walking down along Salt Lick Creek to emerge on Wildernest's Buffalo Drive or farther to Wildernest Center. To do this, return on the Lily Pad Trail to the irrigation ditch. The Salt Lick Trail heads downhill east from here through a pretty drainage dotted with beaver ponds. When you reach the first large ponds, cross uphill at left. Look for a cabin ruins just beyond. The trail connects to a road, then junctions at the beginning of a pine forest with several other trails. Use the signed Placer Trail to come out at Buffalo Drive, a total distance of 4.5 miles. Or, continue down the dirt road to emerge at Wildernest Center, another 0.5 miles.

Salt Lick Gulch became the scene of an 1860s gold strike when Summit County pioneer, Edwin Carter, shot a deer and discovered gold particles in the animal's teeth. He tracked the animal to Salt Lick Creek and discovered gold there! Carter, a naturalist, later built a taxidermy collection that began the Denver Museum of Natural History.

Salt Lick, mined heavily in the early 1900s, saw its hillsides washed down by forceful streams of water from giant nozzles and hoses. The "pay dirt" from this 160-acre venture was then washed to retrieve gold.

Ski touring: *(Easy)* Ski the Lily Pad Trail roundtrip to the snow-covered lakes. Or cruise down through Salt Lick Gulch on a 4.5-mile tour as described above. (Rated *More Difficult* due to a few steep tight turns in the trees.) Note the irrigation ditch path, a raised, curving, snow-covered track. The Salt Lick route heads downhill for a good starting schuss, then drops through meadows and trees in a smooth downhill glide. Since no blazes mark the first section of trail, watch for natural signs of the route. Fortunately, Salt Lick is popular with skiers, so tracks, or snow-blurred track depressions, will help to guide you down. Skiers can use the free bus to ride back uphill. Call 668-0999 for schedules.

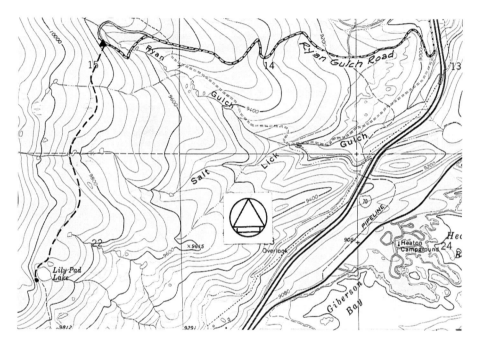

Fur trappers once invaded beaver pond-dotted high forests, like those near Lily Pad, to trap pelts for popular1800s gentlemen's hat.

...the mountains and the hills before you break into singing and all the trees of the field shall clap their hands. Is 55:12

37 BUFFALO MOUNTAIN

Time: 6-8 hours
Distance: 1.8 miles
Elevation gain: 2,977 feet
High point: 12,777 feet
Rating: Most difficult
Usually open: Mid-July-mid-Sept.
Topo: USGS Vail Pass 1970, rev. 1987
       USGS Frisco 1970, rev. 1987

"There is a good cabin at the base of Buffalo in the timber," the April 29, 1882 *Summit County Times* noted. Over a century later, this ruined cabin points the way to a trail climbing 12,777-foot Buffalo Mountain, a challenging scramble with special rewards. A full 360-degree vista west beyond Vail, south toward Hoosier Pass, east to the Divide and north along the Williams Fork Range climaxes a hike superabundant in its views.

Before you begin this hike, take a look at Buffalo from Dillon or another good spot where you can see the mountain's domed east face. The Buffalo Trail goes through forest on the lower right (north) slope of the mountain, climbs the sparsely-forested avalanche path clearly visible above and emerges from timberline to curve southwest on rubble rock up to the summit. The route remains right (or north) of Buffalo's glacial cirque and gully. The trail does not show on the maps. Wear firm shoes for the rocky summit.

Drive north on Colorado 9 from Silverthorne I-70 exit 205 to the Wildernest Road, across from Wendy's. Turn left by the 7-11 store and proceed 3.3 miles to the top of Wildernest to the marked trailhead for South Willow Creek and Buffalo Mountain. Park.

The trail rises northwest from 9,800 feet altitude through a pine forest. Before long, reach a primitive road climbing west. Leave the South Willow Trail and follow this road to a half-cabin in the trees. A footpath begins beyond the cabin at 10,400 feet to start you on the Buffalo trek. This steep trail climbs to the Buffalo Mountain avalanche path, where it becomes indistinct.

If you happen to lose the trail in the snowslide area, just keep going up and you will do fine. If you keep the trail, note its location when you leave the trees so that you can pick it up easily on the return trip.

On the loose rock near Buffalo Mountain's crest, no trail exists. Stay well right of the glacial cirque, with its hidden hanging lake. A number of false summits can discourage hikers on this strenuous climb. The actual summit is a narrow rim on Buffalo's curving half-dome. The mountain's west side drops in a sheer pitch to a wet, green valley below.

Rest stops along the way allow ever-expanding views of Lake Dillon, the lower Blue River valley, Frisco and the Continental Divide. Marsh marigold, columbine, wild rose, lupine, harebell and many more flowers grow along the wooded portion of the trail. Buffalo has no tundra, just shard rock above timberline, but we saw a single columbine plant with a dozen blue blossoms, blooming in a sea of broken gray granite.

Silver once seamed Buffalo's imposing granite hulk. The Buffalo Mountain Silver Mining Company tunneled the mountain's north shoulder in 1881. Buffalo's Winona, Chicago, Wildcat, Hancock, Garfield and Washington were lode claims worked from four tunnels, the longest penetrating the mountain's rocky flank 130 feet. Miners unearthed silver, lead and gold in "pay streaks" as wide as 40 feet.

Below, the Wildernest subdivision lies on two large early-day placer claims, the North Side and the Poplar. A number of smaller placers nearby took names from the fermented juice of the noble grape--Burgundy, Tokay, Claret and Sauterne.

Buffalo Mountain looked like that animal's curving back to early settlers. Strange as it may seem, buffalo once roamed the Blue River valley, grazing on abundant grasses, especially north of Silverthorne. Nomad Ute Indians used buffalo meat, skins, organs, horns, sinew and just about everything else in their daily life.

Prominent Buffalo Mountain can be seen from practically everywhere in the county. Early miners may have named gold rich Buffalo Flats (Breckenridge Golf Course) for its good view of the mountain as well as the buffalo grazing there. From the Keystone Lodge bar, from high on Pennsylvania Creek above Breckenridge, from the Dillon stoplight, from just below the Eisenhower Tunnel, locals and visitors view old Buffalo. For that reason, it is rewarding to have stood on its summit!

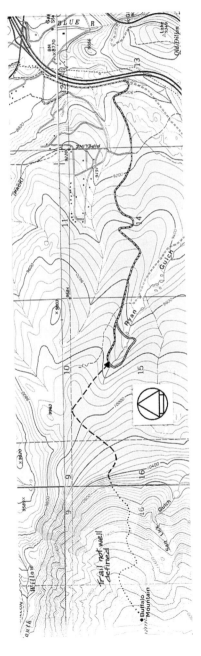

Eyeball Buffalo Mountain route before doing the climb. Path ascends through trees to avalanche path on right, then crosses southwest to summit.

38 MESA CORTINA

Time: 3 1/2-4 hours
Distance: 2.6 miles
Elevation gain: 380 feet
High point: 9,600 feet
Rating: Easy-moderate
Usually open: June-Sept.
Topo: USGS Dillon 1970, rev. 1987

A fun place for kids, a refreshing place for friends to stroll, a nice place for a picnic, the Mesa Cortina Trail is pleasant and relaxing. While the up-and-down forest path has a stretch rising 400 feet in 0.7 miles, it generally offers an easy walk and a delightful ski tour.

Drive Colorado 9 north from I-70 Silverthorne exit 205 to the Wildernest Road at the 7-11 store corner across from Wendy's. The trailhead is in Mesa Cortina, 1.6 miles. Turn left and proceed to the fork. Turn right, then immediately left onto Royal Buffalo Drive (No. 1240). Drive 1.0 miles to Lakeview Drive (No. 1245) and turn right. Proceed to a fork with Aspen Drive. Go left on Aspen, up and around a short distance to the trailhead pull-off.

The trail begins near private homes in Mesa Cortina, where the big Royal Red Bird and Royal Buffalo placer mining claims, each near 60 acres, once dominated the area. The path winds through aspen forest to two sagebrush-and-grass meadows with views of the Blue River Valley and Silverthorne, Ptarmigan Mountain and Lake Dillon, dotted white with sailboats in summer. On several moms-and-kids hikes here, we have watched bounding deer, captured baby frogs in the ponds below the trail and picnicked in the summer meadow. Children also enjoy learning about the aspen forest by touching the tree's elephant-hide bark, watching its leaves "quake" in the breeze, smelling the damp, musty scent of a dense aspen stand and understanding the aspen community's interlocking root system, connected beneath the soil. In autumn, look for the aspen wood's palette of color from sunny-yellow and gold to salmon and cerise. These colors vary from year to year, depending on moisture, sunshine and soil factors. Children can hunt for "horsey trees" in the aspen forest. These bent aspen, almost horizontal, bounce like buckin' broncos when kids pretend to ride them.

Wild iris in June, then harebell, mariposa lily, columbine, cinquefoil, lupine and wild rose bloom on the Mesa Cortina Trail.

The path enters the Gore Range Wilderness at the edge of a lodgepole forest and climbs on switchbacks under dense tree cover. At 2.1 miles the trail merges with an early-day road rising from the old Emore Ranch, a pioneer family's homestead now developed as the Ruby Ranch. Another half mile brings you to South Willow Creek, a good destination for a relaxed hike. Signs here give mileages for points on the Gore Range Trail. South Willow, one of three rushing creeks that drain the Red Peak area, begins behind 12,777-foot Buffalo Mountain, below its steep west drop-off. The creek tumbles down between Buffalo and 13,189-foot Red Peak, sometimes cascading in waterfalls (see hike No. 39).

Ski touring: *(Moderate)* Skiers will enjoy the abundant snowfall in the Mesa Cortina-South Willow district. Summit County's first newspaper, launched in 1879, described two miners who first attempted to winter here. Mr. James Murdoch and Mr. John P. Scarff witnessed "250 inches of snow (twenty feet, 10 inches)", according to the April 29, 1882 *Summit County Times.* Twelve foot-long by four-inch wide miners' skis, with a single six-foot steering and braking pole, kept Scarff and Murdoch from succumbing to cabin fever.

Ski the hiking trail, which remains a clear route despite winter snows. Watch the fast drop as you approach the ranch road. You may wish to extend the tour beyond South Willow Creek, at 2.6 miles, to a high meadow at 3.3 miles. A rustic cabin, long a landmark here, burned in 1981. The meadow, at 9,560 feet, makes a good turn-around point. Steep slopes of Buffalo and Red close in ahead, threatening avalanche.

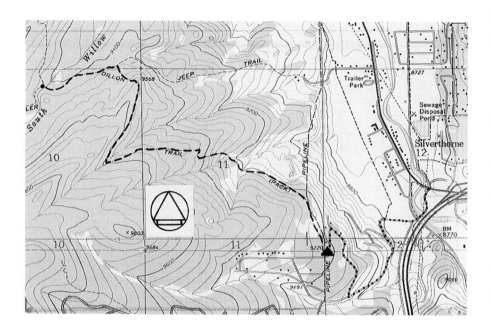

Aspens nourish wildflower soil with fallen leaves. Mesa Cortina Trail's vibrant aspen colony provides great photo opportunities.

Ample snowfall blesses Mesa Cortina Trail with conditions sure to please skinny skiers.

39 SOUTH WILLOW FALLS

Time: 4-5 hours
Distance: 4.3 miles
Elevation gain: 980 feet
High point: 10,200 feet
Rating: Moderate
Usually open: Mid-June-Sept.
Topo: Trails Illustrated Vail-Frisco-Dillon

Four silvery waterfalls, plus a seltzer-fizzle chute, plunge over mammoth rocks at the South Willow Falls. Visitors will delight in their power and natural beauty.

Drive to the Mesa Cortina trailhead using directions for No. 38.

Earlier editions of *The Summit Hiker* used the South Willow trailhead in Wildernest to short-cut the trip to the falls. But this trail has deteriorated into a labyrinth of confusing trails from overuse. Mesa Cortina is a good alternative--longer, but faster to walk.

The trail traverses splendid meadows, then penetrates dark pine forest to emerge in the deep gorge between Buffalo Mountain and Red Peak. The Mesa Cortina Trail meets the Gore Range Trail at 2.6 miles, where the route crosses South Willow Creek. You will now join the Gore Trail heading west-southwest (go straight ahead) and continue beside the tumbling creek into a rich forest.

Wildflowers here include some rarities: The delicate pink fairy slipper, a native orchid, blooms here along with more common purple larkspur, blue columbine, white brook cress, yellow lousewort, wild roses and many more.

Hikers will climb on the Gore Trail, an aspen-lined path. A huge rock at trail's left provides a foretaste of the mammoth stone formations that are the hiker's clue to arriving at the waterfalls area. Look for these and a trail that cuts off to the left. Take this left trail a short distance to the falls.

A half cabin, former cabin site and mine ruins here may have belonged to the D. S. Dow & Company camp near the head of South Willow in 1882. Miners wintered in the area for the first time that year and reported 250 inches of snow, with 10, 20 and 30-foot depths in canyons and coves. Twelve-foot long by four-inch wide miners snowshoes (skis) insured "no serious trouble for either snow or cold", the 1880s-published *Summit County Times* reported.

An early day visitor to the sparkling waterfall was Ruby Lowe, whose historic homestead became today's Ruby Ranch development. Though Ruby served for years as Summit Schools superintendent, her leisure time delight was to ride a favorite horse to South Willow falls or northwest to Salmon Lake.

Both children and adults enjoy exploring around the waterfalls. Climb the rocks, soak tired feet in an icy pool, hunt for the water cave or just picnic by the crystal cascade.

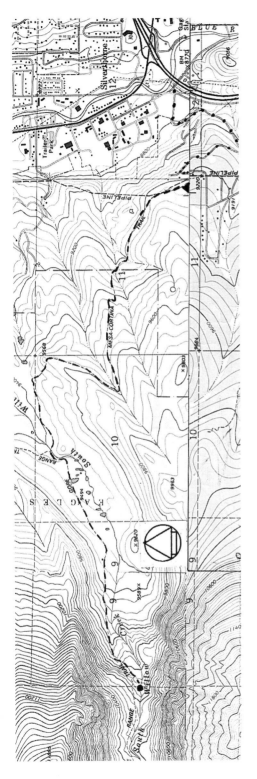

Cool off at South Willow waterfalls where older kids can enjoy walking on massive rocks.

40 RED BUFFALO PASS

Time: 8-9 hours
Distance: 15.7 miles
Elevation gain: 2,520 feet
High point: 11,740 feet
Rating: Most difficult
Usually open: July-mid-Sept.
Topo: Trails Illustrated Vail-Frisco-Dillon

A demanding all-day hike with dramatic views, Red Buffalo Pass gets you to Vail the "quick" way. Interstate 70 highway designers seriously considered this pass rather than the meandering Vail Pass route. Heavily tramped by miners' boots a century earlier, this historic byway, formerly called Wilkinson Pass, remains remote, untrodden and beautiful.

Two cars are required. Leave one car at the Gore Creek Campground, 6 miles east of Vail: Follow I-70 west from Frisco and cross Vail Pass. As you descend the pass, the campground will be on your right, but no direct access from I-70 exists. Instead, proceed to the East Vail exit and double back left on the frontage road to the campground. The trail snakes up a grassy hillside, beginning about 50 yards north of the campground entrance.

Drive a second car to the trailhead in Mesa Cortina, following directions for hike No. 38.

The trail rises gradually through meadow-pocketed aspen forest, then pine, to meet, at 2.1 miles, an old ranch road. Columbine, lupine, wild rose, harebell and the more rare mariposa lily grow here, as well at the red elegant columbine and unusual varieties of the violet. Native orchids sometimes blossom in the Wildernest-Mesa Cortina area as well. August brings many kinds of mushrooms, while September unleashes a splash of gold.

At 2.6 miles, meet South Willow Creek and the Gore Range Trail junction. Stay left.

This pleasant route, with rock outcroppings and unusually large pines, climbs to a sun-bathed meadow at 3.3 miles. Just above lies the intersection with the South Willow Trail from Wildernest and beyond that, at 4.2 miles, a short trail leading left to the commanding South Willow Creek Falls, a great rest stop at 10,200 feet. Note the massive rock formations here. Scan the mountain sides for mine tunnels.

Steep jagged slopes of Buffalo Mountain, left, and Red Peak at right, form a big crevice as the trail continues. After the falls, the valley opens up to a delightful garden of Indian paintbrush. Then a thick pine forest encloses the trail. Later the path curves south to intersect at 6.2 miles with the Gore Creek Trail from east Vail. (The Gore Range Trail crosses the big green alpine bowl, dotted with shining ponds, to mount Eccles Pass to the south.) This hike will go right, scale Red Buffalo Pass and cross to the Gore Range west slope. Be sure to veer right; many hikers lose the way here. Look for yellow glacier lilies early season.

At the head of South Willow Creek in this bowl, an 1800s miners colony bustled. The 1882-discovered Wildhack Mine, a silver lode, belonged to long-time Frisco postmaster Louis A. Wildhack. D. S. Dow & Company and Greenlee & Company also mined here.

Red Buffalo Pass, 11,700 feet, provides a falcon's view of the Gore Range and a long sweep into the broad Gore Creek valley leading to your Vail destination.

The Gore Creek Trail switchbacks from the grassy slope at the crest, down to cross Gore Creek, passing a ruined cabin, a rock cairn and grassy meadow enroute. Shorter switchbacks follow the creek crossing, then the trail emerges from the woods to enter a large meadow at the edge of a basin. Stay left (southwest) and look for trail signs. Drop at a moderate grade through the woods. A large open area and two smaller clearings follow, then the trail crosses Gore Creek. A log 20 yards downstream may keep your feet dry.

A sign indicates Gore Willow Creek Pass before you veer left and walk to the Gore Lake Trail junction. Look for a grave, less than 50 yards from the creek crossing, which commemorated 1870s Summit County pioneers, the Recen brothers. Early Ten Mile

Canyon silver discoverers, they founded the town of Recen, which merged into old Kokomo, an 1880s boom town.

Another mile brings you to a large treeless section along the valley wall. Soon drop through woods and pass small, stagnant ponds. Cross Deluge Creek. The trail descends from evergreen forest to grass and aspen woods, crosses a few shallow streams, then drops down to the Gore Creek campground, a long, but rewarding, walk.

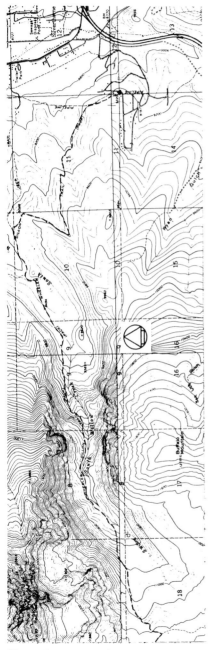

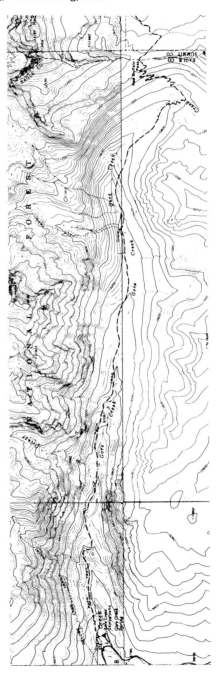

Map continues in next column.

95

41 WILLOW LAKES

Time: Overnight trip
Distance: 8.5 miles
Elevation gain: 2,180 feet
High point: 11,400 feet
Rating: More difficult
Usually open: Mid-July-mid-Sept.
Topo: USGS Summit County 1978 (2 sheets)
    or Trails Illustrated Vail-Frisco-Dillon

Four pristine lakes, perched on the steep north slope of Red Peak, form jewels on the strand of upper North Willow Creek. Their dazzling neighbor, Salmon Lake, is set in a magnificent mountain amphitheater.

Drive north on Colorado 9 from Silverthorne exit 205 to the Wildernest Road at the 7-11 store, across from Wendy's. The trailhead is in Mesa Cortina, 1.6 miles. Drive a short distance to a fork and go right, then immediately left onto Royal Buffalo Drive (No. 1240). Turn again at 1.0 miles, right onto Lakeview Drive (No. 1245). Proceed to its fork with Aspen Drive. Go left on Aspen, up around a curve to the trailhead parking area beyond.

The Mesa Cortina trail joins the Gore Range Trail at South Willow Creek (2.6 miles), then climbs to meet the Willow Lakes Trail (6.1 miles) leading to Salmon and Willow Lakes.

(An alternate access, beginning at Rock Creek, shaves 1.3 miles from this hike's length and 300 feet from its elevation gain. However, this forest-enclosed trail offers less variety. Use directions for Rock Creek (No. 42). Walk 0.3 miles from the trailhead to its intersection with the Gore Range Trail and turn left (south) for a 4.8-mile walk to the Willow Lakes Trail junction. Total mileage on this route is 7.2 miles.)

The trail meanders through an aspen wood, with fluttering wildflowers on the forest floor, which enhances the path's rolling first section. Meadows open up views of Silverthorne and Lake Dillon. The trail enters a dense lodgepole stand and climbs to level out in dry pine forest. Now go left on a closed road from the old Emore Ranch (today's Ruby Ranch development). At 2.6 miles. cross South Willow Creek and a trail junction. The Gore Range Trail, coming from the north, turns here to climb west toward Red Buffalo Pass. Follow the Gore Range Trail north (a right turn). It takes you across the lower flanks of 13,189-foot Red Peak where 24 silver mines operated in the 1880s, toward the mountain's lake-studded north slope.

Six creek crossings keep you nimble-footed as the trail follows a fairly level route. The first four streams feed Middle Willow Creek. This area, characterized as "busy as a hive" in 1882, buzzed with the activity of the Colomar Mining Company operating near "the center of Middle Willow". A log headquarters here was surrounded by prospectors' tents "from June to October", early newspapers reported. Mines in this area included the Highline Chief, Silver Vault and Bellwether. Two branches of North Willow follow, then the trail curves northwest to parallel North Willow Creek. After another mile or so, the path begins a steady climb. Reach the Willow Lakes Trail junction, a left turn, at 10,800 feet elevation and 6.1 miles. A sign nailed to a tree may mark the path. The trail will treat you to views of an impressive pyramid hikers call "The Thorn" or "East Thorn".

Now a stiff one-mile climb takes you to view meadows before you reach the Salmon Lake cut-off, a confusing fork. If you miss it, just listen for water running under the rocks, a noisy clue to the stream flowing from Salmon Lake. Go 250 yards to the lake.

Salmon Lake, glass-smooth against the rugged backdrop of 13,333-foot East Thorn, hugs timberline at 11,200 feet. A few big spruce may survive nearby but "alpine" is clearly the character of this lake in its splendid granite amphitheater.

Return to the junction and choose the left fork for Willow Lakes. The first of four Willow

Lakes, 0.6 miles farther, appears at trail's left. These mountain lakes glisten below the spectacular, spired Zodiac Ridge, a skyscraping salute to the Creator.

The trail fades before the far lake, 8.5 miles. Most campers choose one of the two larger lakes. Eagles Nest Wilderness rules permit campsites over 100 feet from a lake, but no closer. Firewood has diminished here. Moreover, ecological concerns persuade campers to use a gas stove for cooking. Water, on the other hand, is in ample supply.

Explorers might hunt for the Silver Vault Mine, a rich silver lode located "on Red Peak in the Willow Lakes area at the head of North Willow Creek", according to early Summit County mining claim records.

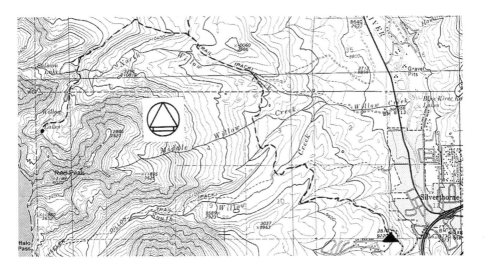

Turrets of the Zodiac ridge frame the high Willow Lakes set in a bowl north of Red Peak. Eagles Nest residents can connect to the trail to the lakes via Middle Willow Creek.

42 ROCK CREEK-BOSS MINE

Time: 1 1/2-2 hours
Distance: 1.5 miles
Elevation gain: 680 feet
High point: 10,200 feet
Rating: Moderate
Usually open: Mid-June-Sept.
Topo: USGS Willow Lakes 1970, rev. 1987

Historic Rock Creek, with remnants of the 1880s Naomi ghost camp at its confluence with the Blue River, offers a satisfying short hike to a once-booming silver mine. Along the way, the trail penetrates a bird sanctuary, a no-cost concert of chirpy song.

Drive 7.3 miles north from Silverthorne on Colorado 9. Watch for the Blue River Campground sign to loom up on the right. Just before you reach the sign, turn left onto a dirt road, the Rock Creek Road (No. 1350). Proceed along this road, veering left at the fork. (Avoid the right fork leading to private property with no forest access.) Stay on the main road for 3 miles to the Arapaho National Forest Rock Creek Trailhead parking.

The trail begins on the road at left, not the footpath from the parking area. Walk to a gate. The old Boss Mine ore wagon road, used in later years by jeeps, is closed to motorized vehicles beyond this point. The 1880s road, smooth as a parkway, continues 1.5 miles to a large mine site.

Notice the Gore Range Trail intersection at 0.3 miles. The hike to Boulder Lake (No. 43) uses this path northbound, while the alternate access to Willow Lakes (No. 41) uses the southbound branch. A sign announces the trail's entry to the Alfred Bailey Bird Nesting Area, developed in cooperation with the Denver Field Ornithologists. Alfred Bailey served as director of Denver's famous Museum of Natural History. Common Western bird species are protected in the sanctuary, one of a kind in Colorado when established in 1973.

A string of more than a dozen beaver ponds near the road makes a pleasant picnic spot on a summer's day.

Stay right when the trail forks. Soon the trail climbs alongside a steep wall as you near the Boss Mine. The rugged high ridges of Keller Mountain, unseen before, materialize above. Look for an old shaft and hoist house hidden among the aspens above the trail at right. Square nails date the construction to pre-1900s.

A barren mountain of gray mine tailings dominates the view as you approach trail's end. The Boss, Josie and Thunderbolt Mines operated here on North Rock Creek from silver's discovery around 1881 to well past the turn of the century. During the early years, miners lived in the 1880s town of Naomi, below at Rock Creek's mouth, and used horses and pack mule trains to transport themselves and their ore over the nearly 5-mile route from the mine. In June, 1897, the *Denver Republican* reported the Boss and Thunderbolt had produced nearly $500,000 in silver ores (today's dollar value--$3,500,000).

Mine machinery lies scattered about on the tailings. A neatly notched log building constructed with wooden pegs stands here along with a second building ready to collapse. Mining buffs can explore the tailings and enjoy the Gore Range views.

When you return to Highway 9, pull off at the old road entrance just south of the Rock Creek Road. This area, protected by fence and a guard dog, is Naomi, the old Blue River stage roadstop where the 1870s-built Naomi hotel served travelers and miners. Harry Forche, Dillon postmaster, quit his job to run the hotel and a postoffice at Naomi. Later a general store opened. The Gould brothers built a sawmill at Naomi to cut ties for a Denver and Rio Grande rail route down the Blue, but the railway plan fizzled.

Ski Touring: *(Moderate)* Rock Creek offers a wonderful cross-country ski experience. Use the driving directions above, but proceed 1.4 miles to the winter trailhead. Ski on a gradual climb through aspen-pine forest along North Rock Creek. At one point the trail splits but later joins again. The trail rises for about 1.6 miles to the signed summer parking area, then passes the gate to open meadows and bird sanctuary above. Total distance to the Boss Mine is around 3 miles. Watch for unstable snow in the upper meadow.

The 1880 town of Naomi, a stage stop on the Dillon-Kremmling coach route, stood for many years at Rock Creek's mouth.

Massive tailings dump at Rock Creek's once-prosperous Boss Mine mounds below Keller Ridge. Trail served as mine roadway.

43 BOULDER LAKE

Time: 3-4 hours
Distance: 2.4 miles
Elevation gain: 480 feet
High point: 10,000 feet
Rating: Moderate
Usually open: Mid-June-Sept.
Topo: USGS Willow Lakes 1970, rev. 1987

A rippling high country lake with a rugged mountain wall as a backdrop nestles amid pines on beautiful Boulder Creek. A great spot to picnic or overnight, the lake trail makes a short hike suitable for families, on a path that rises and drops from the Rock Creek trailhead.

One drawback: Wet summers can make low spots on this trail miserable. Extra footwear for children may be necessary.

An alternate trailhead exists at the end of the Boulder Creek Road, No. 1376, which lies just north of Rock Creek. However, local dogs are territorial and parking is illegal on this road (cars must have all four wheels *off* the roadway), so this book recommends the Rock Creek access.

Drive Colorado 9 north from Silverthorne using the Rock Creek auto and trailhead directions (No. 42).

The trail follows the old Rock Creek mining road for 0.3 miles to its junction with the Gore Range Trail. Turn right (north) onto the Gore Trail, which ascends to a lodgepole forest. The footpath undulates, crossing low areas that become mud bogs during rainy periods. Pass several small ponds and negotiate large stones to cross a couple of little streams. A closed trail leads downhill right to Pebble Creek and restricted private property.

Although this route receives heavy use on weekends, traffic normally quiets down midweek. On the day we chose Boulder Lake for a quiet stroll, the path came alive with 40 Outward Bound trail runners who gasped "on your right" or "coming through, please" as they slipped and slid over wet stones on a demanding run from Rock Creek.

After 1.8 miles on the Gore Range Trail, cross Boulder Creek and head uphill along the stream's right bank, just 0.3 miles to lower Boulder Lake. A less-defined trail climbs the left bank as well. A noisy, tumbling watercourse, Boulder Creek provides moist conditions for many streamside plants. Marsh marigolds grow here in June and raspberries ripen in September.

The lake, at 9,800 feet, offers good exploring, especially for kids supervised by adults. A trail on the lake's right (north) shore climbs several miles southwest through dense forest with deadfall and bog to a smaller upper Boulder Lake at 11,240 feet. The trail often disappears.

Return to Rock Creek via the Gore Range Trail. This impressive 54.5 mile trail traverses the east slope of the Gore from near Eaglesmere and Mahan Lakes north in the Cataract region to 0.5 miles above Copper Mountain at its southern terminus. The Wheeler Trail begins just south of Copper and continues another 15 miles or so to Hoosier Pass. Almost 70 miles of trail connects Summit County's boundaries on two paths that rise and fall across creek bottoms and ridges, through heavy secluded forest and open-vista alpine meadows.

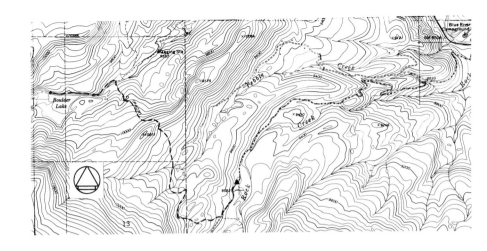

Saw-tooth Gore Range peaks guard pine-rimmed Boulder Lake, popular hikers' destination.

44 GORE RANGE TRAIL

Distance: 54.5 miles
High point: 11,900 feet
Rating: Moderate
Usually open: Mid-June-Sept.
Topo: USGS Summit County
         (North) 1978 and (South) 1976

Rolling and winding across the forested flank of the magnificent Gore east slope, the 54.5 mile Gore Range Trail travels from Summit County's far north near Mahan Lake above Green Mountain Reservoir to Copper Mountain at its southern extremity. (From there, the Wheeler Trail continues, crossing the Ten Mile Range to the Hoosier Pass area and county line.) The entire trail remains within the Eagles Nest Wilderness.

The Gore Range Trail, maintained in a primitive state, has its share of rocks, roots and bog to challenge the hiker. However, excellent signage, provided by the U.S. Forest Service in recent years, reduces to almost nil the possibility of getting lost. The trail rises and falls for most of its impressive length, passing through montane, sub-alpine and alpine life zones. Its low near Black Creek lies at 8,800 feet in aspen-pine forest, while its high soars to a treeless 11,900 feet at Uneva Pass. Most of the trail traverses conifer forest at around 10,000 feet.

A footpath nearly all its length, the Gore Range Trail has nine gateway points listed with this guide's hike number to facilitate reaching the access. They are:

Mahan Lake	Brush Creek	Meadow Creek (18)
Eaglesmere (48)	Rock Creek (42)	North Ten Mile (16)
Surprise (46)	Mesa Cortina (38)	Copper Mountain (19)
		(Wheeler Lakes)

Hikers can walk the trail in sections. Following are these sections, U.S. Forest Service mileage figures for each, topographic maps needed and a brief trail description:

Mahan Lake junction to Eaglesmere:
4.5 miles   USGS Summit County (North) 1978
Starting at 10,800 feet, this trail section winds under the spectacular pinnacle of 13,432-foot Eagles Nest mountain, a rewarding walk despite trail bog.

Eaglesmere to Surprise:
3.0 miles   USGS Summit County (North) 1978
Sparkling streams, dramatic rock formations and two lakes make this section exciting. Eaglesmere Lake lies a short distance off the trail, but Tipperary and Surprise Lakes are almost trailside. Go left at a confusing fork before reaching rushing Cataract Creek.

Surprise to Brush Creek:
6.5 miles   USGS Summit County (North) 1978
The trail crosses Otter Creek and the road to Blue and Black Lakes, just before reaching Black Creek, the Gore Trail's 8,800-foot low point. This beautiful creek tumbles down from Black Lake where General Albert H. Jones, a civil war veteran, stocked trout and built a picturesque cabin in early days. A good climb out of this drainage brings you to the first of two trails to Lost Lake.

Brush Creek to Rock Creek:
10.5 miles   USGS Summit County (North) 1978

Look for elk and deer between Brush and Squaw Creeks. The Palmer Ranch, just below, belonged to a long-time Summit ranch family headed by Irish-born Isaac Charles Palmer who came to Breckenridge in gold rush days. Open meadows and views, along with seven creeks to cross and many trailside ponds, mark this more level section. The path curves beneath Guyselman Mountain, named for a local rancher and judge. (A 0.3 mile trip up Boulder Creek to Boulder Lake is a nice rest stop.) The trail rises and falls to Rock Creek, crossing some boggy areas.

Rock Creek to Mesa Cortina:
10.6 miles   USGS Summit County (North) 1978 and (South) 1976

Deep forest closes in, providing few views, but hikers had better watch the trail anyway, for rocks and tangled roots threaten firm footing. Cross two Rock Creek branches early on, then no water until North Willow. A trail to the Willow Lakes intersects at 4.8 miles. The path seems long until you reach the several Willow Creeks and drop into aspen forests above Mesa Cortina.

Mesa Cortina to Meadow Creek:
6.25 miles   USGS Summit County (South) 1976

See Red Buffalo Pass (No. 40) for trail description. Veer left at 11,400' to Eccles Pass.

Meadow Creek to North Ten Mile:
3.0 miles   USGS Summit County (South) 1976

A beautiful meadow at 11,200 feet leads to a forest of enormous trees and a steep 1,000-foot drop into the canyon.

North Ten Mile to Copper Mountain:
10.0 miles   USGS Summit County (South) 1976

Climb 800 feet in 0.7 miles, then mount Uneva Pass, 11,900 feet, this trail's highest point. Try a side trip to Wheeler Lakes (No. 19).

The Gore Range Trail takes its name from a well-heeled Irish huntsman, Sir St. George Gore, who launched a luxurious 1855 safari here to slaughter for sport a generation of game--2,000 buffalo, 1,600 elk and deer, 100 bear, numberless antelope, small game and fish. Lord Gore had 28 vehicles, a portable tent-manor and a fur-lined commode!

Handsome wooden bridge spans North Rock Creek, surprising hikers on rugged 10.5 mile Gore Range Trail between Rock Creek and Mesa Cortina access points.

45 LOWER CATARACT LAKE

Time: 1 hour
Distance: 2 miles
Elevation gain: 100 feet
High point: 8,730 feet
Rating: Easy
Usually open: Early June-Sept.
Topo: USGS Summit County (North) 1978

A great summer outing, often a bit too popular, lower Cataract Lake nestles deep in a forested valley, a mountain lake pretty as anyone could ask. The loop trail encircling the lake crosses sunny sagebrush meadows to enter an icebox pine forest, then follows a hillside for an expansive view of the lake. When most Summit trails remain in snowmelt, Cataract opens in June. Visit mid-week or after Labor Day for less crowded conditions. And expect a $5 fee per auto to visit the lake during peak months.

Drive 16 miles north from Silverthorne on Colorado 9. Turn left onto the Heeney Road (No. 30) and proceed 5.3 miles to County Road 1725. Turn left and drive 2.3 miles to a fork past the Cataract Creek Campground. Go left past the Surprise trailhead and park.

The trail makes an elongated loop around Cataract Lake, so you can begin at left, or go right, past the green gate to the signed trailhead. Starting left, walk a level path on the south bank. Look for a huge tree, nearly dead with a trunk diameter of almost five feet. Summit County's virgin forest, before its destruction by early prospectors, had many large trees, but a gold rush building boom, logging, forest fires and railroad track construction denuded large forests. Since trees grow slowly in high altitude conditions, few like this one remain.

Massive flat rocks form a path to a bridge over Cataract Creek. Cataract plunges into the valley from a cliff above, creating a roaring waterfall. Miles above, one of the advanced hikes (No. 47) follows a creek fork to upper Cataract Lake.

Crossing shard rock at 8,600 feet is unusual--it's normally found at higher altitudes. Later, in a boulder-strewn area, curious diamond drill holes appear in the rock, a puzzlement to hikers. The holes remain from drilling during trail construction to prepare for blasting.

Listen for the birds, many varieties, which populate aspen glades on the lake's north side. A Forest Service administrative center overlooks the lake in an idyllic spot. The trail soon ends, having taken you through a variety of ecosystems from sagebrush meadow to mossy pine forest to lichen-covered rock hillside, back to the meadow where cows munch the grass.

The lake's beauty has attracted a horde of enthusiasts who unwittingly trample the natural beauty they come to admire. The Forest Service has recently directed campers to stay 500 feet from the lake.

Cataract Lake served as the destination of an early-day road that climbed four miles from the ranches on the lower Blue River below. Before Green Mountain Dam (1942), this "best flatland grazing area in the county" ranked as prime ranching land, from the 1880s on. The federal Homestead Act gave disgruntled miners a chance to start anew in the peaceful valley. Where Green Mountain Reservoir lies now, the historic Knorr, Mumford, Laskey and Marcott Ranches once spread. George Mumford, an 1860s Buffalo Flats prospector, owned an impressive 650 acres in placer mining claims near Breckenridge by 1882, before he homesteaded his Cataract Creek ranch. A school, built near Knorr's small lake in 1902, was called Lakeside. The Lakeside Hall became the scene of dances, parties, church services and elections, a social center for a ranching community that raised hay, cattle and, on Saturday nights, high hilarity.

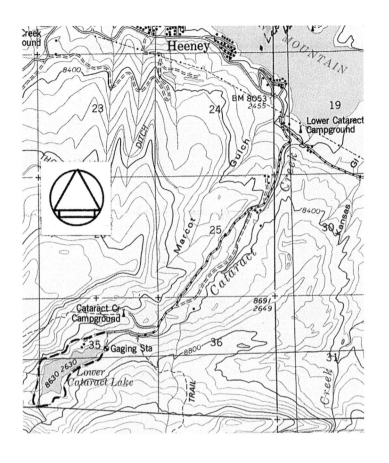

A survivor from Summit's pre-1860 virgin forest, huge tree interests hikers on Cataract Lake Loop.

46 SURPRISE AND TIPPERARY LAKES

Time: 5-6 hours
Distance: 2.6 and 5.0 miles
Elevation gain: 1,840 feet
High point: 10,400 feet
Rating: More difficult
Usually open: June-Sept.
Topo: USGS Summit County (North) 1978

Hiking is great exercise. The aerobic hike to Surprise and Tipperary Lakes will upgrade your heart-lung efficiency and firm your flab. Rewards for this healthful endeavor are two forest-rimmed lakes, both unbeatable places to cool tired feet and munch a vegetarian lunch.

A word about maps: The USGS maps published prior to 1978 show incorrect features of this and other trails in the Mt. Powell area, so be sure to carry a recent map.

Drive beyond the Cataract Creek Campground using directions for hike No. 45. At the fork, go left and park near the trailhead sign for Surprise, upper Cataract and Mirror Lakes. Cross the bridge over Cataract Creek.

The trail climbs a grassy slope winding up through aspen groves and flowery meadows. Ford a shallow stream at 0.7 miles. Where a faint path goes left, stay right.

When the footpath connects to an old road, the trail begins to rise relentlessly, quite steep in spots, into a pine forest. At a little over 2.0 miles, meet the Gore Range Trail. A Forest Service sign marks the trail which makes an acute angle right turn to Surprise and Tipperary Lakes. You reach the 10,000 foot mark on the short walk along the Gore Trail to Surprise Lake on your left.

Surprise, at 9,920 feet altitude, blossoms with butter-yellow Indian pond lilies on its northwest shore during late July-early August. The mountain lake makes a good rest or lunch stop. If you choose to make Surprise your trail's end, you have hiked 2.6 miles one way with a 1,440-foot elevation gain.

Continue west on the Gore Range Trail for an hour's hike to Tipperary Lake. The footpath crosses a stream, a tributary of roiling Cataract Creek, then meets the upper Cataract Lake Trail (No. 47). Upper Cataract, and Mirror Lake beyond, lie on an advanced trail that ultimately reaches Elliott Ridge, the 12,000-foot crest of the Gore Range and the Summit County boundary.

Heavy pine forest closes in as you climb to 10,400 feet, the trail's high point, then drop to the lake elevation of 9,760 feet. You can see Tipperary from the trail, on your right. A path descends to the lake, which perches on a steep pine-covered slope plunging to the Cataract valley.

On your return, note the Grandview Cemetery next to a fisherman parking area on the Heeney Road just before Colorado 9. Ulysses Grant McKinley, a local rancher, established the graveyard on his property after a tragic accident took several lives. A horse shied crossing the Blue River bridge near here and plunged McKinley's carriage into the Blue, a raging river during those early years. Children and adult relatives on the Sunday family outing drowned in the rushing river. Some burials are marked, with local ranch family names like McKinley, Smith, Marcott, Guthrie and Wyatt, while others are unidentified stone-ringed graves.

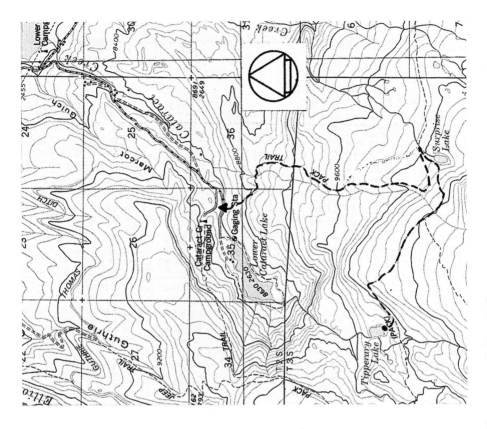

Blue Valley rancher, Ulysses Grant McKinley, established modest Grandview Cemetery after a tragic accident. Visit graveyard on return from Surprise trailhead.

47 UPPER CATARACT, CAT AND MIRROR LAKES

Time: 8-9 hours
Distance: 5.5 and 6.6 miles
Elevation gain: 2,280 feet
High point: 10,840 feet
Rating: Most difficult
Usually open: Mid-June-Sept.
Topo: USGS Summit County (North) 1978

The undisturbed beauty of the primitive Eagles Nest Wilderness comes alive on a rugged hike high into the Cataract Creek drainage. Two clear lakes below 13,432-foot Eagles Nest provide a pleasant destination on a trail offering long views down to the Cataract Valley.

Drive to the fork beyond the Cataract Creek Campground using directions for hike No. 45. Go left at the fork to the trailhead parking area. The hike starts on the Surprise Lake Trail.

The trail begins beyond the bridge crossing Cataract Creek. A path climbs to meet the Gore Range Trail, which passes Surprise Lake and leads to the upper Cataract Lake Trail. This route traverses Eagles Nest's north slope to Mirror Lake. The trail's eventual goal is soaring Elliott's Ridge where it joins an exciting ridgetop route along the Gore crest.

Beautiful aspen groves alternate with grassy meadows as the trail rises more than two miles to reach the Gore Trail. Ford a shallow stream at 0.7 miles. When a faint path leads off right, go left. When the path turns into rugged roadway, begin climbing sharply in conifer forest. Some sections here are surprisingly steep!

Turn right onto the Gore Trail and cross the 10,000-foot level on a short walk to Surprise Lake on your left. Look for yellow Indian pond lilies in late July and early August along the lake's northwest shore. After a breather at Surprise, continue on the Gore Trail as it rises another 400 feet to cross a stream. Beyond it, about 150 yards, is the Cataract Trail. Turn left (west) here.

Now the trail climbs southwest for about 2.0 miles before dropping from 10,840 feet, the trail's high point, down along switchbacks to the lake.

The creek links Cataract Lake to its serene sister, Cat Lake, below the trail. To reach Cataract, cross a large boulder field that stands between trail and lake. You will arrive at the rocks above the water. Note the junction for the short trail to Cat Lake here. Turn left and walk about 200 yards to the northeast Cataract shore. A headwall behind the lake rises to 13,099 feet, with a tiny lake hanging on a high ledge. Cataract, at 10,760 feet, can be your destination (5.5 miles) or you can go on to Mirror Lake.

The track clings to the steep north slope of 13,432-foot Eagles Nest Mountain nearing Mirror Lake. When the trail crosses Cataract Creek, you are there--but hikers often lose the path at the creek. Elongated Mirror Lake lies below at left, a short distance past the crossing. This lake, at 10,560 feet, usually lives up to its name and reflects its surroundings. Cataract Creek, which feeds Mirror, has its head near Elliott's Ridge, above at 11,800 feet.

If you have extra time, consider an alternate route down. A 10-mile loop trail that meets near lower Cataract Lake, uses the Eaglesmere and Surprise Trails as links to the Gore Trail, which connects the two. You can turn left on leaving the Cataract Trail, travelling the Gore Trail north. It passes Tipperary Lake, the 10-mile loop's midpoint. Then the path continues another 5 miles through rugged, rocky (and fairly level!) terrain to a stunning descent along an open hillside above lower Cataract Lake. Views extend across the valley and beyond to the Williams Fork Range. The trail ends a short distance above your parking area. Walk the road down to your car.

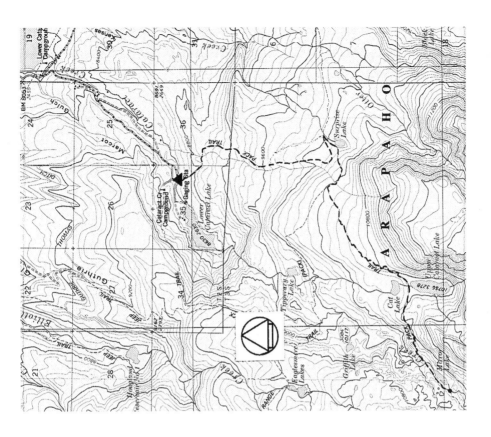

Rustic ranch building reminds Cataract hikers of lower Blue Valley's history as a ranchland community. Some longtime families still remain.

48 EAGLESMERE LAKES

Time: 5-6 hours
Distance: 3.3 miles
Elevation gain: 1,700 feet
High point: 10,420 feet
Rating: More difficult
Usually open: Mid-June-Sept.
Topo: USGS Summit County (North) 1978

"Serendipity" means a special kind of happy surprise. The word suits Eaglesmere, where sumptuous views unfold as the trail rises along an open ridge. These heights unveil the tranquil beauty of Cataract Lake, at repose in a rich, forested valley with the Williams Fork mountains beyond.

Drive Colorado 9 north from Silverthorne using directions for hike No. 45. Along County Road 1725, note the typical weathered ranch buildings at roadside. When you reach the fork above the Cataract Creek Campground, proceed right 0.2 miles to park.

Several cows grazed near the Eaglesmere trailhead on our first hike in 1982. When we revisited in 1991, we were dismayed by erosion from cattle trampling in the meadow above the ridge. The Forest Service has granted grazing rights in this pristine area. By 1997, the permit holder had agreed to remove the herd from the trail area. Because the Eaglesmere Trail excels in scenic beauty, we declined deleting it from *The New Summit Hiker* (as timber cut-ravaged Gold Hill was cut from this edition). Instead, we encourage hikers who note problems to write the Forest Service, Box 620, Silverthorne, CO 80498.

The trail heads off into aspen glades alive with bird song. The breeze stirs the rippling aspen and releases their scent, making this section of the trail a delight to the senses.

Climb along the shoulder of a steep hillside for wonderful valley views. Ute Pass and 12,303-foot Ute Peak in the Williams Fork Range rise above the quiet Blue valley. Listen for Cataract Falls' muffled roar as it tumbles below 13,432-foot Eagles Nest Mountain.

The trail maintains a steady climb. Soon enter a meadow of tall grass, then pine forest closes in, heavy, dark and green. Quickly, the trail opens again in a sunny meadow, then dappled aspen woods. A view across the valley to Tipperary Lake emerges.

Flowers, abundant on this lower-altitude trail, include the white-blossoming serviceberry shrub (also called Juneberry and shadberry--used by the Indians for pemmican), pasque flower, wild rose and sunflower. Rare ferns, including Bracken's fern, grow here. Autumn walks are glorious.

In deep forest at 2.8 miles, the Eaglesmere Trail meets the Gore Range Trail, marked with a sign. Turn right (west) onto the Gore Trail and walk to the next junction (unmarked) where you turn left for a short southbound hike to the two Eaglesmere Lakes.

The first lake, the smaller, is separated by a land strip from the second. Snow-capped Eagles Nest dominates the view from the larger lake.

Ranchers whose land spread along lower Cataract Creek where it met the Blue River (beneath today's Green Mountain Reservoir) used trails like Eaglesmere for hunting, trapping and fishing in trout-filled high lakes. Heavy winter snows isolated these ranch families, restricting their diets. But in summer, fishing holes and hunting grounds, high-altitude gardens, mountain gooseberry and chokecherry patches, along with raising pigs and chickens and making homemade ice cream from the thick, rich cream of local dairy cows, provided plenty of variety. Summer was a busy time for ranchers, however. Birthing, branding, feeding, herding and selling cattle, plus planting, cultivating and harvesting hay, made summer work a dawn-to-dark job.

Hikers interested in a ten-mile-plus circle tour can return to the Gore Range Trail and follow it east past Cataract Creek, Tipperary and Surprise Lakes to the Surprise Trail. Use that route to drop down to the Surprise trailhead and a short uphill walk to your car.

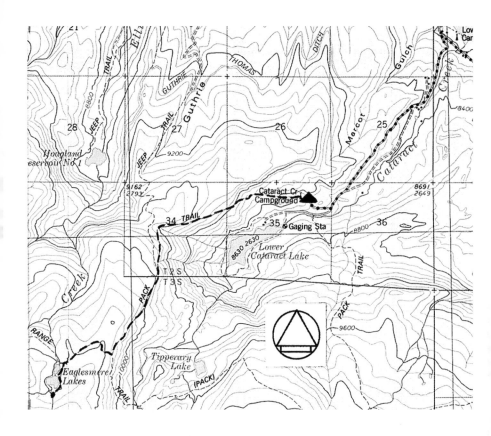

In serene contrast to the exhilarating views from the Eaglesmere Trail is peaceful, rock-rimmed Eaglesmere Lake. An isthmus connects the two lakes. The far lake offers splendid views of Eagles Nest Mountain. Rare Bracken's fern, found on trail, has a Latin name meaning "like an eagle's wing". Look for soaring birds.

Hikes in the Williams Fork Range

49 UTE PEAK

Time: 6 hours
Distance: 5 miles
Elevation gain: 3,255 feet
High point: 12,303 feet
Rating: Most difficult
Usually open: July-Sept.
Topo: Trails Illustrated Green Mountain Reservoir Ute Pass

Launched near scenic Ute Pass, this rigorous hike offers several possibilities: High-energy hikers can climb steep 12,303-foot Ute Peak for its glorious 360-degree views. Backpackers can continue the hike to Silverthorne along the magnificent crest of the Williams Fork Range. Exit from this longer hike via either the Ptarmigan Trail (17.6 miles) or Laskey Gulch (17.1 miles). Leave a second car, if you choose the hike to Silverthorne, at either the Ptarmigan or Laskey Gulch trailheads See hike 34 or 35 for driving directions.

The statistics listed above refer to the Ute Peak climb only. Please note that the USGS map misrepresents the trail's location. Trails Illustrated matches the actual route walked with a GPS system much closer but still misses the trails junction at 9,900 feet. Bring water when hiking to Ute Peak and beyond. Quiet hikers may glimpse the area's wildlife.

Drive 12 miles north of Silverthorne on Colorado 9 to the Ute Pass Road (No. 15). Turn right and travel 5.2 miles to a parking area at left, just west of the cattle guard before the pass summit. Park, cross the road and walk across a meadow to the woods where a trailhead sign is posted.

Hikers will use two trails to reach Ute Peak. First, the Ute Pass Trail begins below aspen-covered hillsides that light up with gold in autumn. The path crosses into Grand County and forks at 1.9 miles. There the Ute Pass Trail drops into the Williams Fork River drainage while this hike's route, the Ute Peak Trail, cuts back west to the William Fork Range crest.

The trail passes two cattle gates. Close them to protect grazing stock. Leaving the aspen behind, the path penetrates a moist, cool pine forest. Green is everywhere, with leafy ground cover, moss and flowers carpeting the forest floor. Marsh marigolds bloom early in summer, then lupine, blue chimingbell, harebell and columbine in mid-summer and purple gentian in September.

A confusing choice faces hikers at the stream crossing. Go left. Where the trail forks again at 9,900 feet, a sign indicates the Ute Pass-Williams Fork route, left, and the Ute Peak Trail, a sharp-angle right turn. Go right. Ignore the sign's mileage number. You are 1.9 miles in on a 5 mile trail. The trail now climbs south, then swings sharply west before a steep section beginning at 2.3 miles. This leg is tiring and unrewarding. But after you complete the last final dip and climb above timberline at 11,100 feet, superb views unfold.

The trail turns south for a tough 1,000-foot-plus climb with a steep final scramble up Ute Peak. The southernmost bump is the real summit. There the Gore Range spreads a feast of views before you as you stand on the Summit-Grand County line. Just below, west across the Blue, lies Slate Creek where some of Summit County's best parties took place at the old Slate Creek Hall. The building remains in use today. The beautiful Lund Ranch, homesteaded by a Danish immigrant family, became a popular spot for winter Sunday ski outings by local ranch families. Rancher Charles Lund, who first attended the tiny Slate Creek schoolhouse as a little boy whose family spoke little English, maintained the working Slate Creek Ranch until his death in 1982.

Among the Gore Range peaks visible are Eagles Nest, 13,432 feet; Dora Mountain below it, 12,292 feet; Mount Powell to the south, 13,448 feet; and Guyselman Mountain, 13,213 feet, named for Judge William Guyselman, a Holland-born immigrant who came to Breckenridge to practice law and homesteaded a Cataract Creek ranch in 1881.

Hikers enroute to Silverthorne will follow the ridge south-southwest for 8 more miles to Ptarmigan's summit or 9.3 miles to Ptarmigan Pass atop Laskey Gulch. Views of the Gore and Ten Mile Ranges, along with the Continental Divide mountains east, are spectacular.

From Ptarmigan Peak, follow the 4.6-mile Ptarmigan Trail down (see No. 34 for directions). From Ptarmigan Pass, follow Laskey Gulch 2.8 miles to I-70 (see No. 35).

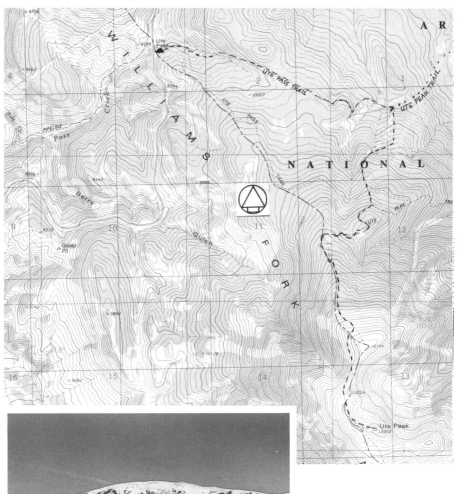

Snowslide-striped Ute Peak provides staggering views to the Gore and beyond.

May the Lord rejoice in his works.
Ps. 104:31

50 ACORN CREEK

Time: 3-4 hours to lower ridge/5 hours to upper ridge
Distance: 2.5 miles/ 3.4 miles
Elevation gain: 1,768 feet/2,560 feet
High point: 10,400 feet/11,200 feet
Rating: More difficult/ Most difficult
Usually open: Mid-June-Sept.
Topo: USGS Ute Peak 1980, rev. 1987
     USGS Squaw Creek 1980, rev. 1987

Flowers galore and views aplenty characterize Acorn Creek, where it's hard for hikers to yank their gaze from the July wildflowers to the commanding peaks of the Gore. Two destinations provide walkers a choice between an invigorating and a rigorous hike.

The trail offers a variety of ecosystems. Begin in sagebrush dappled with mariposa lilies; enter pine forest purple with lupine; cross meadows of delphinium; then wind through aspen glades fluttering with blue columbine. If you miss the late-June to July flower season, choose September for brilliant aspen color.

Drive Colorado 9 north 10.7 miles from Silverthorne I-70 exit 205 to Ute Park Road, No. 2400. Turn right. Follow the road onto Rodeo Drive, then to the Acorn Creek trailhead at 1.0 miles. Walk to the parking lot's south end, beyond the raised berm, to the path.

The trail crosses a meadow to a gate in a barbed wire fence. Close the gate to protect livestock. Views at the start provide a dazzling sample of more vistas waiting high in the Acorn Creek valley. Follow a stock drive trail leading to a footpath. Veer left on the trail twice, then again go left to cross the creek on a log bridge. (Avoid a false trail right here.)

Alternate through trees and meadows, entering the Ptarmigan Peak Wilderness at 2 miles. Advance to the first ridge, called "the sheep camp," where the path meets a side trail to form a T. Go left and enjoy the panorama. This ends the moderate hike, a 2.5 mile walk to 10,400 feet.

Continuing hikers advance on switchbacks that become steep and gravelly. A good boot and hiking poles come in handy here. Remarkable views accompany you to the Williams Fork ridge top at 11,200 feet. There, meet the Ute Peak trail and go right to view a glade of gaunt tree skeletons, an unusual sight, at this hike's end. The ridge trail continues 12.6 miles south to Silverthorne, 1 mile north to Ute Peak and 6 miles north to Ute Pass.

The historic Acorn Creek Ranch once spread across both North Acorn and Acorn Creek's lower drainages. The 1,324-acre property began with 160 acres homesteaded in 1885 by Thomas Marshall, a stagecoach driver on the Como-Leadville route. Marriage united the Marshalls to another pioneer family, the Mumfords. George Mumford placer mined near Breckenridge in the 1860s and '70s before homesteading a ranch on Cataract Creek. Angus steers and hay provided the mainstay of the near-century-old Acorn Creek Ranch. Family descendents still work the property today.

Across the valley lies another homestead, the Slate Creek Ranch, developed by a Danish immigrant family, the Lunds. Homesteads comprised 160 acres but ranchers soon learned they had to expand to survive. The Lund Ranch grew along with Slate Creek, which had its own school and the Slate Creek Hall, scene of many lower Blue Valley box supper socials, parties and dances (and a few Hatfield-McCoy-type feud brawls as well).

Ski touring/Snow shoeing: *(Moderate)* Begin in a big, snowy meadow above the trailhead for an Acorn Creek ski outing. Use the gate to head up through a cut in the trees. Enjoy supple aspen, deep green pine and snowy open meadows. Choose the north side hiking route for your tour or explore the southern route. On the south fork you'll reach a "Private" sign. Stay left (east) of the fence. Continue through three drainages. At Quaking Aspen Creek turn right and ascend a powder meadow. Use this sunny meadow for a ski picnic and enjoy the Gore Range's panorama of wild ridges and peaks.

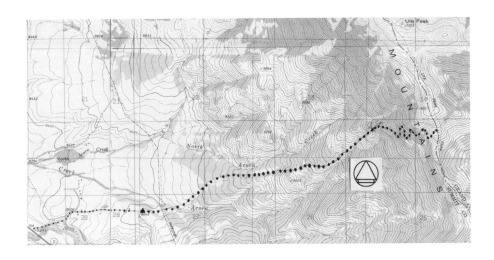

Enter the Ptarmigan Peak Wilderness at 2.0 miles. Its lush meadows contrast with the fire-and-wind sculpted tree skeletons atop the stunning ridge at the hike's end. Wildlife officials ask Acorn trail users to avoid visiting early season when elk calve here.

Get FREE Postage on three or more books

————THE NEW————
SUMMIT HIKER
AND SKI TOURING GUIDE

50 Historic Hiking Trails

A Creative Gift: For any outdoor enthusiast's library.
Accurate: Unmatched trail descriptions.
History-rich: Mining, ghost towns, narrow-gauge railways.
Ski Touring & Snow shoe Guide: 22 scenic ski trails.
Completely Revised: Expanded to 50 historic hikes.

Discover Summit County's Lively History!

SUMMIT
A Gold Rush History of
Summit County, Colorado

Crazy characters...ghost towns...Ute Indians...narrow-gauge railways...mine camps...348 pages.. more than 100 antique photographs... a lively, well-written gold rush history.

We endorse this historical look backward at Breckenridge's rich past and that of Summit County as a whole...
The Breckenridge Centennial Commission, Inc.

Order from Alpenrose Press, Box 499, Silverthorne, CO 80498. Please use coupon on page 118 to order.

·THE·
VAIL HIKER
·And Ski Touring Guide·

New! 50 Scenic Hikes

View Stunning Scenery and Wildlife
Discover Mining and Ranching History
Explore the Unspoiled Holy Cross Wilderness
Enjoy the Primitive Eagles Nest Wilderness

Get the new edition of this best-selling guidebook, **The Vail Hiker**. Get the data you need: Trail description, time, distance, elevation gain, high point, difficulty rating, season open and suggested USGS topo map. Driving directions to trailheads. Hikes for every level from family to mountaineers.

Order The Vail Hiker, Snowshoe and Ski Touring Guide from Alpenrose Press, Box 499, Silverthorne, CO 80498. Use coupon on last page to order.

VISIT THE GHOST TOWNS with

BRECKENRIDGE!

Explore famous gold mines... discover ghost towns... tour a gem historic district.

15 ghost towns and sites

   12 major mines

      2 gold dredges

         43 historic buildings

           Jeep and auto tours, self-guided walking tours, ski jaunts

Order by mail from Alpenrose Press, Box 499, Silverthorne, CO 80498. Please use coupon on back page to order..

ORDER FORM

Please mail my book(s) to me at this address:

Name: _____

Address: _____

City: _____ State: _____ ZIP: _____

___(Quantity) The New Summit Hiker 16.95 ea.
                Colo. only tax .96

___(Quantity) The Vail Hiker 16.95 ea.
                Colo. only tax .96

___(Quantity) SUMMIT softcover 15.95 ea.
                Colo. only tax .90

___(Quantity) BRECKENRIDGE! 4.95 ea.
                Colo. only tax .28

Postage & Handling @ 2.50 ea. book _____
(3 or more books – Free Postage)

Total Enclosed _____
Check or Money Order Only

Send to: Alpenrose Press, Box 499, Silverthorne, CO 80498-0499

Request Author Autograph!
Please autograph my copy. To:_____
(Name of Recipient)

 Alpenrose Press

THE NEW
SUMMIT HIKER
AND SKI TOURING GUIDE
Trail Map

Legend

⑧ ---- Hiking Trail & Hike Number

▲ Trailhead - Park Here

Stream or River

Road

U.S. Forest Service Office

No. 800 County Road

•••• Continental Divide

┼┼┼ Wilderness Area Boundary

⛷ Ski Area

County Line